DEATHCLUTCH

DEATHCLUTCH

MY STORY OF DETERMINATION, DOMINATION, AND SURVIVAL

Brock Lesnar
with Paul Heyman

WILLIAM MORROW
An Imprint of HarperCollins*Publishers*

All photographs in the insert courtesy of the author, with the exception of:

page 4, top: courtesy of the University of Minnesota
pages 4, bottom; 5; 6; 7; 8, top; 9, top: courtesy of Baseball Magazine-Sha, Weekly ProWrestling/Fumi Saito
page 8, bottom: courtesy of Gregory Davis
pages 9, bottom; 15, top; 16, top: Scott Peterson/MMAWeekly.com
pages 10–11; 14, top; 16, bottom: Josh Hedges/Zuffa LLC via Getty Images
page 13: Jon Kopaloff/FilmMagic
pages 14, bottom; 15, bottom: Jon Kopaloff/Getty Images

HarperCollins books may be purchased for educational, business, or sales promotional use. For information please write: Special Markets Department, HarperCollins Publishers, 10 East 53rd Street, New York, NY 10022.

FIRST EDITION

Designed by Lisa Stokes

Library of Congress Cataloging-in-Publication data has been applied for.

ISBN 978-0-06-202312-4

11 12 13 14 15   OV/QGF   10 9 8 7 6 5 4 3 2 1

CONTENTS

DeathClutch

I **WAS LIVING WITH** a dark cloud over my head for seventeen months. I had gambled every bit of my reputation as a legitimate athlete, and I was determined to erase the stigma of being a WWE entertainer. All I had to do was smash Frank Mir into the ground, but I made a rookie mistake and got caught. These things happen in life, but I'm supposed to be better than that. I handed this guy, who will never be half the man I am, a victory he didn't deserve.

So for seventeen months, I waited.

For seventeen months, I imagined what would happen in the rematch.

For seventeen months, I couldn't wait to get my hands on this guy again and show him, my family, the world, and God what I was capable of.

When the wait was over, I did everything I intended on doing. I beat Frank Mir to a pulp, took him down to the ground, and smashed in his face so bad, the referee had to stop the fight.

I was not only the Undisputed UFC Heavyweight Champion of the World, I had gotten out from underneath that dark cloud that just wouldn't go away.

I was so happy. I found my true calling. I was with the woman I love and am going to spend the rest of my life with. I had moved my parents close and given something back to my mom and dad. My wife had just given birth to our happy, healthy baby boy Turk.

Life wasn't just good, it was great. The best it had ever been. I was never happier.

And then I almost died.

What the hell happened to me? I'm supposed to be hunting and fishing with my kids. I'm supposed to be rewarding my wife for all of her love and support. I'm supposed to be kicking ass, ruling the MMA world, being the Baddest Dude on the Planet.

I'm not supposed to be stretched out, withering away, dying in some hospital in the middle of nowhere, surrounded by a bunch of doctors who can't determine how sick I am because they are waiting on a part for a CT machine to arrive. Even without a proper diagnosis, they want to cut me open.

It's amazing what goes through a man's mind when he's in the clutches of death.

RAISED TO BE A CHAMPION

I WANT YOU to understand something. It's real simple. I owe it all to my mom and dad. Who I am. What I am. Where I am.

Parents put a lot of pressure on their kids to succeed in sports, whether they mean to or not. Some kids can handle the pressure and live up to their parents' expectations. Other kids can't, and they fail. It wasn't like I was being given a choice. I had to win.

I was born with the talent and the athleticism—those were God-given gifts. But a lot of talented athletes go nowhere. What made me different? More than anything else, my mom and dad, and the rest of my family for that matter, were willing to make sacrifices for me.

There are a lot of people who helped mold me into a champion, but my mom and dad deserve the credit first, before anyone else. I didn't grow up with a silver spoon in my mouth. I didn't grow up like a lot of people think I did, as a spoiled athlete who got his ass kissed all the way through school, and was catered to and coddled. I grew up poor, on a dairy farm in South Dakota, and I had to work for everything I have. A lot of my friends were not allowed to play any sports or participate in other after-school activities. They were farmers, and farm chores came first. We were farmers, too. But my mom and dad let me start wrestling when I was only five years old. I milked cows and shoveled manure like everyone else, but I never missed a wrestling practice.

My parents got me into every wrestling tournament they could because they wanted me to learn what it was like to compete. As far back as I can remember, weekends meant wrestling tournaments. I can picture myself in the back of the family station wagon for hours on end, watching the farm fields go by, and wondering where we would end up.

My mom did most of the driving to practices, matches, and tournaments, because my dad had to stay home and work the farm. They both made it whenever they could, but sometimes I had to hitch a ride with another family or my coach. However I got there, my job was to win.

My mom didn't accept any excuses. If I lost, it was my fault. Period. I couldn't blame a loss on the referee, and there were no teammates to let me down. It was just me and the other kid on the mat. One winner. One loser. The outcome was up to me, and me alone.

When I lost a match—as I did from time to time—it was "admit it, accept it, get in the car, and let's go home." My mom's comments were always brief, and she always said the same thing. "There's another match next weekend. If you don't like the way you feel when you lose, then get in there and win. What do you want to be in life? The guy who feels good because he wins, or the guy who feels like you do now because he lost?"

My mom was pretty stiff, but it turned out to be the best thing for me. It may seem coldhearted, but she loved me enough to make me want to go out there and earn victories. Just like crying was not acceptable if I lost, there was no big celebration if I won. Instead, my mom would just say, "Good job, Brock, now let's get in the car and go home. You won. That's what you're supposed to do."

My dad was no different. If I won a trophy, he would say "good job." If I lost, he would tell me to try harder and win the next time. That was it. The expectations were clear. Losing was not an option.

Looking back from where I am now, I wouldn't have had it any other way. Wrestling is a competition. So is life. Even as a kid, I walked into every tournament for one reason—to win. My mom and dad expected no less, and they taught me to never settle for second best. I haven't.

I will never forget how upset my mom was when I lost in the quarter finals of the National Junior College Wrestling Tournament. It was during my freshman year at Bismarck State College in North Dakota. She really wanted me to excel—to stand out. She wanted me not only to live up to my potential, but to do even more. She knew I had been blessed with certain gifts as an athlete, and that I had the ability to push myself harder than anyone else; so why wasn't I number one? In her mind, there was no reason I shouldn't be the best, and she wasn't ever going to let me think second place was "okay."

Sure, my mom pushed me hard to win. She saw a passion in me. She saw that I was a competitor. She wanted me to make the most of my natural instincts. I was her last son.

I was the third of four children, and I feel bad for my siblings because most of the time I was the center of attention. My two older brothers, Troy and Chad, were standout athletes in their own right, but chose not to p   rts as a career. Over time, they became known as Brock's brothers. My poor little   was a very good athlete too, and she excelled at basketball, volleyball, track, and any other sport she decided to play. But no matter how well she did, she still had to live in the shadow of her big brother Brock.

I won't lie. Being the center of attention had its perks. But it wasn't all good. I felt the pressure to succeed, too. What set me apart is that I accepted all challenges.

At a very young age I developed an inner confidence that I still have today. I don't know if it's ego, attitude, arrogance, or something else. But whatever it is, it works for me.

I think my self-confidence is why, for as long as I can remember, I've been the backbone of my family. I am comfortable being the go-to guy. The one people depend on. The one in control. It's always been that way for me. I still try to take care of my mom and dad, and I will always try to make sure the rest of my family is taken care of. That's just who I am. It's up to me, and I look out for the people I love.

At the same time, I know my limitations. I know I'm not perfect. I know what I know, but more importantly, I know what I don't know. When I don't know something, I surround myself with people I can trust to teach me.

How many times have you seen an athlete who is his own worst enemy? He can't leave his ego at the door when he walks into the gym or onto the playing field. Nobody can tell him anything. I never had that problem. Every coach I've ever had, from kindergarten to college to my current MMA coaching team, will agree: I am coachable.

I know to this day that it's so important to have the right coaches around you. A great athlete needs coaches that can see mistakes, work on imperfections, point out what sometimes is the obvious, and motivate. Athletes are too close to the competition, and don't always see things that a coach may see clear as day.

I have been very fortunate to have had great coaches, from my youth and high school coach, John Schiley, to my junior college coach, Robert Finneseth, and my University of Minnesota and current professional coach, Marty Morgan. Those two, in particular, deserve a lot of credit.

The same way my mom made sure that I learned from my mistakes, the nature of the sport of wrestling really brought that lesson home. In wrestling, you can win a tournament one day, and the very next day you might be taken down in the practice room by a B-squadder or a guy who is at the weight below you. That's why wrestling is such a humbling sport, and why it reinforced the same lessons my mom kept teaching me over and over again.

Every day with my parents, and in the gym, was a constant reminder. I'm not perfect. I can always make a mistake. One mistake is all it takes. One, simple, stupid, momentary lapse (like the mental mistake I made in my UFC debut against Frank Mir) is all it takes to go from "champion" to "loser." As soon as you start to think you are too good, that you just can't slip up, someone will always be there to show you the error of your ways.

But I had my mom and dad, and they were behind me all the way. If it weren't for their belief in me, and the sacrifices they made, you would not be reading this book. They are my biggest fans, and I am theirs.

WRESTLING WITH MY FUTURE

FARMING IS THE life I enjoy, and the one I look forward to most when my fight is over. I farm now because I choose to—not because it's all I know. I'm not stuck on my farm. I want to be here. But it wasn't always that way.

When I was a junior in high school, I wanted a future that included something more than milking cows and sitting on tractors. It just happened that as I was thinking about how to get off the farm, a National Guard recruiter showed up at my school. My dad was in the Guard, so I didn't think he'd mind if I signed up. As a matter of fact, I didn't even ask him; I had my mom co-sign for me.

Here I was, seventeen years old, on my way to Fort Leonardwood, Missouri. Let me say this for the record, so that everyone who is reading this can understand something. The nine weeks I spent in the National Guard that summer changed my life. I came back home a totally different person, and all for the better.

The only problem was that I went into the Guard to join the local artillery supply unit. We worked with explosive charges that were coded red and green. That's what I wanted to do. But after an eye test, which showed that I am red-green color-blind, I was assigned to clerical duty. Can you see my big ass sitting at a computer screen all day? That was not exactly what I had in mind when I signed up. Lucky for me, I couldn't pass the typing test, and that was the end of my Guard career.

During guard training, we had to run every morning, which helped me nail a two-mile run in 10:56. When I went back to high school for my senior year, I was in great shape, and I had one more year on the football team with my friends. I even signed a letter of intent to play football at Northern State University in Aberdeen, because I didn't have any wrestling offers.

I wanted to run the ball. I had the speed, and I was getting some size. But just as I was starting to rack up some impressive numbers, a defensive back took my knee out, and I had to have knee surgery. That was the end of my high school football career.

High school wrestling starts when the football season ends. That meant that my knee wouldn't be completely healed before the first day of wrestling practice. In fact, when wrestling started I was still on my crutches.

That was bad enough. But to make matters worse, every year since I was in sixth grade, our coach, John Schiley, made us do a six-mile run on the first day of practice. It was called a "gut check," and everyone was expected to finish if they wanted to be on Schiley's team. This was my senior year and I was a leader. So I started the six miles on crutches and kept going until the coach was satisfied and let me jump in the back of his pickup. I was disappointed, though, because I had finished that run every year since I was in sixth grade.

Believe it or not, I was a late developer. As a young kid, I certainly was no heavyweight. I was a string bean.

In seventh grade, I wrestled at 103 pounds. As a freshman in high school, I was a 152-pounder; sophomore year, I was 160. By my junior year, I was 189 pounds. Finally, as a senior, I made it to the heavyweight division, but only by a couple of pounds.

Looking at me now, it might be hard to believe that I didn't even have hair in my armpits when I graduated from high school. I guarantee you I was the last guy to go through puberty in my class. I lifted a lot of weights, and even though I was a six-foot-tall, 210-pound senior, I still looked like nothing more than a big stretched-out kid. Even in my freshman year of college, at my heaviest, I was only 226 pounds.

Coming up through the high school ranks, I was never a monster by any means. I was just trying to grow into my own skin. But that struggle became a huge positive for me: when I had to wrestle as a 103-pounder, or a 152-pounder, I developed the moves and quickness of a lighter-weight wrestler. When I got to heavyweight, I still had those moves, and I was fast. Had I always been big, I probably would have skated by on strength and size alone, and I never would have learned to move like I do now.

In both my junior and senior years in high school, I placed third in the state tourney. But to me, that was nothing special. I was supposed to win. That's what I came to do.

Even though I only played football in high school because everyone else did, I was still pretty good at it. In my heart, though, I was a wrestler. Football was just something to do with my friends until the wrestling season started.

I never thought of myself as a football player, even when I was exploding through the defensive line. I never for a minute thought I was going to play football in college, or at the professional level. When I looked in the mirror, all I ever saw was a wrestler.

That's probably why, when things didn't work out for me with the Minnesota Vikings, I wasn't all that upset. Instead, in some ways, being the last man cut from the roster only confirmed something I had always known. I can't hide the fact, and I really don't want to hide it. I'm proud to say it: I'm not a football player, I'm a fighter. It's what I do. It's my passion. It's my life.

THE COW-CHIP RECRUIT

IT MAKES ME laugh every time I read one of these articles about how I was a blue-chip athlete and had my ass kissed by recruiters and scouts when I came out of high school. There was no college recruiting war for my services. No under-the-table money. No fancy cars. That's all bullshit. I placed third in the South Dakota state wrestling tournament. That didn't exactly put me on the national recruiting radar.

One thing those articles fail to mention, and what a lot of people don't know about me, is that after high school, I didn't go straight to the University of Minnesota to wrestle at the NCAA Division I level. In fact, I wasn't recruited by any Division I schools, and I almost never made it to the U of M.

Because the big schools were not recruiting me, and because I really wanted to continue wrestling, I started my college career at Bismarck State in North Dakota, a junior college. It was bad enough that I wasn't wrestling in a big-time program; but I only finished fifth at Junior College Nationals my first year. Even worse than the fifth-place finish, though, is that I got beat by a pudgy little kid whose name I can't even remember, and neither can anyone else.

The loss to that pudgy no-name was a major turning point in my life, because there was no way that kid should have been able to beat me. I looked at the guy who won the whole tourney and I knew in my heart I could have beat him for the championship. That killed me, because I never got the chance—the fat kid made sure of that. Sorry I can't remember your name, but I do want to say thanks.

At that moment I looked inside myself, and I got serious. I vowed to be the biggest, strongest, fastest, meanest SOB I could become. I wanted to put on pounds of muscle, train like my life depended on it, and just start crushing everyone. I knew I had it in me, and I was determined to grind through it in the weight room, and on the mat, every day, for as long as it took, until I was on the top. I'm no quitter, and I wasn't going to finish my college career as a loser.

After that first year at Bismarck State, I went home to Webster, South Dakota, for the summer to work and make a little money. My mom and dad helped me as much as they could, but they were poor and just keeping the farm going was draining them. I couldn't call home, and ask my mom and dad to send me money. My mom and dad didn't have the money to give. They did what they could, but it wasn't like the kids I roomed with in the dorms. They had decent cars, cash for food, and money to go out. I didn't have any of that.

When I went back to Webster for the summer break, I knew I had to find a job. My number one goal that summer was not only to make some money, but also to put on twenty-five to thirty pounds of muscle. I didn't want to be a power-lifting meathead guy, one of those big goofy immobile guys who are obsessed about how big their arms look when they wear a T-shirt that's too tight (although I did check out my pythons in the mirror from time to time). That just wasn't me. I wanted to be an athlete: strong, quick and explosive.

I have to tell you, it was a great summer. I worked as a laborer for the REA power company in Webster. Every day, I packed my own lunch, and worked from eight in the morning until three in the afternoon. Then I would go work out with my buddies, Jason Nolte and Troy Knebal. We just pounded the weights. I was determined to bulk up, but at the same time to be a better overall athlete. So I not only went after the weights like an animal, I stretched. Yeah, I stretched! I kept my body flexible and mobile.

Every night we hit the gym at five-thirty. No excuses. It was an obsession. Sometimes, we'd drive to other gyms just to shake it up, keep it interesting, keep the blood flowing. But we never missed a day.

I think that all of my drive, my passion to get bigger, faster, and better comes from the mentality of bring a wrestler. I'm not talking about a pro wrestler, although that requires enormous discipline and sacrifice as well. I'm talking about the lifestyle of an amateur wrestler.

Amateur wrestling is not just a sport, it's a lifestyle. You breathe it, like air. The lifestyle consumes you. As soon as you get up, your first thought is about the fuel you will put in your body. Then you hit the road and do some roadwork, because you want that blood flowing, you want to get that cardio where it needs to be. Always one more mile, one more step. You attack the weights like you're a man dying of thirst, and you're thinking that it will always take one more rep to bring some water up from the well. Then you go to bed, exhausted, and get some needed rest so you can get up and do it again, day after day.

Today's athlete is bigger, stronger, and faster than ever before. They train harder, and they train smarter. No longer can a guy rise to the top of any sport on talent alone. The winners are the ones who train right and are willing to sacrifice the most. The good news is that I had the passion, I was willing to listen to my coaches, and I was always willing to work harder and longer than anyone who wants to take me on.

My work that summer paid off. I went from 226 pounds to 258 pounds. I was flexible, and I was fast. I put on muscle because I had great genetics—my dad and brothers are all big guys—and I ate a lot of beef, drank milk by the gallon, ate bananas by the bundle, and worked my ass off in the gym.

All the time I was training I kept thinking about the discipline I had learned on the farm, and how important it was to follow through on my plans. I knew I could do it, and I did. As a matter of fact, before I went back to school, I believed that I could do anything I wanted in life.

In my sophomore year at Bismarck State, I wrestled in the Daktronics Open at South Dakota State, and I beat the defending two-time national NCAA Division II champion, Ryan Reisal. Next, I went to the Bison Open at North Dakota State University, and I steamrolled through the heavyweight tournament. That's where University of Minnesota head coach J Robinson, and his assistant coach Marty Morgan, first saw me.

The Bison was the first big tourney of the year, and a lot of the guys who went there had to work some of the rust off, because they'd been out in their nice little cars and enjoying themselves all summer. Not me. I had been in the weight room and in the gym all summer, so I had no rust. I came in looking to hammer anyone that stepped on the mat with me.

One of the star athletes for the U of M was a heavyweight named Shelton Benjamin. A two-time All-American for Minnesota, Shelton was no joke, and J wanted to build on Shelton's success and create a great heavyweight team. I was part of that plan.

Next thing I knew, I was on a plane headed to Minneapolis on a recruiting trip. I remember my junior college coach, Robert Finneseth, telling me not to sign anything, but when I got to Minneapolis it just felt like home. The U of M didn't waste any time, and I signed with them that day.

I still had a full season of junior college wrestling ahead of me, but I knew what I wanted for myself and I could see it happening. I went 36–0 that season and won the National Junior College Athletic Association Championship.

Here's a bit of trivia for you. I was the last guy to ever wrestle for Bismarck State College. They shut down the wrestling program after my last year there.

My sophomore year was over, I was the NJCAA Champion, and I was headed for the big time to wrestle for the Gophers. Or so I thought.

A DETOUR ON MY ROAD TO THE NCAA HEAVYWEIGHT CHAMPIONSHIP

THE U OF M coaches, Marty and J, wanted me to move to Minneapolis right away when I finished junior college so I could start working out with their heavyweights, like Billy Pierce and Shelton Benjamin. But, as always, I didn't have any money, and I couldn't afford a place in Minneapolis.

That's where Alan Rice came in. He was a former Olympian, and he was a huge Minnesota Gophers booster. He also happened to own a frat house on campus. Alan said there was an extra room in the attic, and he would rent it to me for dirt cheap, something like a hundred dollars a month. It sounded like a great deal to me.

Let me tell you, if Rice would have charged me twenty cents a month for that flophouse attic, it still would have been too much. It was absolutely horrendous. When Rice said the room was in an attic, he wasn't kidding. This was not some bedroom above a frat house; it was really a stinking attic. I had pigeons up there. It was dusty. It was cramped. It was drafty. I was living in a miserable attic in Minnesota!

To pay the rent for that frickin' place, and to get some money for food, I took a job as a demolition man with a construction company. That was the perfect job for me. Every day from 7 A.M. till the middle of the afternoon, I demolished things with a sledgehammer. And when I was done swinging the sixteen-pounder, I still had time to make my afternoon workouts at the gym.

Yeah, I was paying my dues, but I knew it would all be worth it. I was determined to win an NCAA Division I title, and I was willing to do whatever it takes to get there. The U of M was a program on the rise, and I was going to be its star. But then the road took an unexpected turn.

Just as I was settling into my routine, J Robinson called me and said there was a problem. They were trying to get me enrolled at the U for the fall, but my junior college transcript was twenty-four credits shy of the minimum for eligibility to transfer. Are you kidding me? I was pissed. All I could think was, "You guys had all my transcripts and you saw what classes I was taking. I'm nineteen years old. You're the wrestling coaches. This is something you should have seen right away." But there we were, sitting in J's office, and he's telling me I am twenty-four credits short.

Can you believe that?

After all that I had been through, I wasn't about to just kiss my dream good-bye. I wasn't going to let the system beat me. I was going to take control of my own destiny. Unfortunately, summer sessions had already started at most schools.

J wanted me to go somewhere that had a wrestling team I could practice with, and he had a connection at Lasson Community College in Susanville, California, where the team was pretty good. The original plan was for me to go to summer and fall at Lasson, then transfer to the U. I thought it was a huge move going from the farm in South Dakota to the big city of Minneapolis, even if it is only a couple hundred miles away. But California? J might as well have told me I had to move to Japan. They were both a world away as far as I was concerned.

I immediately went back to my attic in the frat house, grabbed all my stuff, and headed home to Webster. On the way, I was thinking about how to tell my parents that I wasn't a U of M Golden Gopher, and that I was heading out to California in two days.

I never did think of a good way to deliver the news, so I just told my mom and dad straight out, "I'm not eligible for college, and I need to get some quick credits at a school in California." They looked at me like I was nuts, but my mind was made up. If this was what I had to do to get on the U of M wrestling team, then this was what I would do. There was no discussion.

I left home in my ten-year-old Mazda RX-7 with Lasson Community College in Susanville, California, as my destination. I remember thinking this might actually be a really fun road trip.

I didn't know anything about the school I was going to. I didn't know where I would stay. I didn't know how I would afford to eat or where I'd train. All I knew was I had a long drive to Susanville, and by the time I got there, I would be just in time for classes.

I remember driving until I hit Salt Lake City, Utah, around 5 A.M. on a Sunday morning. I pulled into a truck stop and took a little nap, but I knew that if I didn't get my ass back on the road I couldn't get my school credits. And without the credits, I couldn't get into the U of M wrestling program. How could J Robinson not have known I was twenty-four credits short?

I finally got to Lasson Community College at 5:30 A.M. on Monday—the day classes started. I immediately tried to call the wrestling coach. Of course, no one answered—only farm boys would be up at five-thirty in the morning. So I left a message and sat by a pay phone just waiting for it to ring.

I don't know if I was sleeping, or half sleeping, but at around 7 A.M. the phone rings and it's the coach. He says he'll meet me up at the school in a half hour. I was completely exhausted after the cross-country drive, but those damn credits were calling me.

When I met with the coach, he asked if I had any relatives at all in the state of California. If I did, I could register as a resident. It just so happened I had two aunts in California. So I used one of their addresses, and sixteen credits were only going to cost me $160. This was still a lot of money to me, because when I got to California I had exactly $480 in my pocket, and nothing in the bank.

I spent $160 on tuition, which left me with $320. I knew I was going to have to eat, so I put a $200 deposit down on the school food program. That got me breakfast, lunch, and dinner in the dining hall every day, and left me with $120 to spare. But that California school wasn't a great fit for me. I stood out in that place like a big infected sore thumb.

I had my tuition and meals taken care of, but the whole adventure would be pretty pointless if I didn't pass my classes, and that is hard to do without any books. But if I would have paid for all the books I needed, I wouldn't have had any money left over for anything else. So I shared books with the other wrestlers. Sounds easy enough, but I really hated having to bum books off the guys all the time.

Still, Susanville, California, will always be a special place to me. I almost started my fighting career there.

I found a little gym that had some weight-lifting equipment and a mixed-martial-arts dojo. This was my first MMA training. One night, the guys at the gym were all going to Reno, Nevada, for a fight. I called up J Robinson and let him know I was planning to fight in Reno to pick up a few bucks. He told me flat out that I would be jeopardizing my chances at becoming a D-I athlete if I did. That was all I needed to hear, and I didn't go. Had I gotten a taste of MMA fighting back then, who knows? Maybe I would never have gone back to school.

Someday, I'd like to take my wife and kids to Susanville, just for the hell of it. Maybe even make the drive. Show my kids where I had to go, what I had to do, to just make it to the University of Minnesota.

I'm not complaining. I'm glad I paid my dues and earned my own way.

After my California summer, I just needed another eight credits to get enrolled at the U of M. I called my U of M advisor and asked if she would help me make sure all my credits from California got transferred back to Bismarck State College. Then I drove from Lasson to Bismarck and started the fall semester at my old school. But BSC didn't have a wrestling program anymore, and I knew I had to do something to keep up my conditioning and skill level.

Because I had no one to wrestle with at BSC, I drove out to the University of Mary, an NAIA (National Association of Intercollegiate Athletics) school just outside Bismarck, and practiced with their team every day.

Being an overachiever, I took twelve credits that fall, even though I only needed eight. I wasn't taking any chances this time around.

At BSC, I was living with my old friend Mike Eckert, who was my dorm neighbor the year before. Mike was really cool. Same old story: I didn't have any money at all, so Mike shared his room with me. It was just a pad we could crash in, but that was important to me because I had nowhere else to go. I'm just glad that I get this chance to tell everyone what Mike did for me that fall.

I quickly fell into a routine at BSC. Weights in the morning. Back-to-back classes. Wrestling practice with the University of Mary team. Homework. But, every day, all I could think of is that I was one day closer to joining the U of M Golden Gopher wrestling team. I wanted that U of M singlet and all that went with it.

I finished up the semester at BSC and passed all my classes. Then I left school two weeks early so I could get to Minneapolis before Christmas break, because I wanted to get ready for the next semester at the U of M. I also wanted to meet the guys, because I was going to be placed on the team immediately.

When I got to Minneapolis, I moved in with Tim Hartung and Chad Kraft, and those guys really sacrificed for me. The U of M needed a big new heavyweight, so a lot of people went out of their way to help me out. Times were good, and I was headed in the right direction. I was finally living my dream. I was in my first tournament as a Gopher, and lost to Trent Hynek in the semi-finals at the Omaha Open. Welcome to NCAA Division I.

I lost. And it burned my ass. Here I was, the guy who was telling everyone that I was going to be the NCAA Division I Heavyweight Champion. I was the focus of the team. The poster boy. I was supposed to be the star heavyweight. And here I was, in my first tournament, and I lose. It was embarrassing as hell.

I only lost twice that year, that first tournament and my last. In the NCAA finals, I lost to Stephen Neal 3–2. Today, Neal plays right guard for Tom Brady and the New England Patriots, and he wears two Super Bowl rings. Back then, he was the returning NCAA heavyweight wrestling champion.

I lost the match to Neal because he was better than me that day. It was a lesson for me. Never give an opponent too much respect. I believe to this day that if I had just come at Neal full throttle, I would have won the 1999 NCAA finals. But I did learn from my mistake.

I had so much respect for Neal. He was the NCAA National Champion. It changed the way I approached the match. It took me off my game. I thought he was better than he really was. I thought about that 3–2 loss a lot, and I finally realized that I was never going to win the biggest prizes by showing that kind of respect to any opponent again. Not ever. If someone wants my respect, they better beat it out of me. That's the only way they'll get it.

The loss to Neal made me think back to those tournaments when I was five years old, and how disappointed my mom was if I lost a match. I hated to let her down, and I hated the feeling that comes with losing. I was embarrassed when I lost in my first big-time college tournament to Trent Hynek, but this was worse. I went through all this shit, California—back to BSC, borrowed books, borrowed wrestling partners at the University of Mary—just to get on the team at the University of Minnesota . . . and then I lost my biggest match.

I hear all these people say, "It's such an honor to make it to the finals, you should feel privileged just to be able to compete at such a level." That's a lot of bullshit. I'm a competitor, and I learned from John Schiley when I was five years old that you compete to win. I am either number one, or I am a loser. And losing sucks.

I hated losing to Neal. If you think I was consumed with getting that loss back from Frank Mir during my professional career, you should have seen me after I lost in the finals of the 1999 NCAA Division I Wrestling Championships. I had one more year to make my dreams come true, and at that moment I made up my mind that I was going all the way. There wasn't a college wrestler on the planet who was going to stop me.

SENIOR YEAR: ONE LAST CHANCE TO GO OUT ON TOP

FROM THE DAY I walked off the mat at the 1999 NCAA finals, all I could think about was becoming the 2000 NCAA Heavyweight Champion. I went to class, because I had to stay eligible to wrestle. But aside from that, every waking thought was on the big prize. If I ate something, it was to build me up so I could win the title. If I lifted a weight, it was with that ultimate goal in mind. If I stepped on the mat in practice, it was to win, and to win convincingly, regardless of the drill. Winning the Heavyweight title wasn't the biggest thing on my mind—it was all I ever thought about.

When I was throwing 280-pound heavyweights around the mat, the U of M wrestling program was getting some big publicity, and it was all centered around me. Here I was: tall, blond, and chiseled. I was tossing opponents like no one had ever seen before at the college level. The media ate it up, and we were packing the house for every match.

People were coming to see me wrestle, and I enjoyed putting on a show for the fans. However, I really could have lived without the media attention. I actually began to hate it.

I found out very quickly that I could manipulate a lot of people and create a lot of interest in upcoming matches based solely on the words that came out of my mouth. But it wasn't an act, it was just me. I was raised to speak my mind, and I did.

If you look back, you can find a *Minneapolis Star-Tribune* story from 1999 that reported a comment I made about what I was going to do to Wes Hand, the Iowa Hawkeye heavyweight, and how the U of M was going to steamroll over Iowa. Just because I made that comment, we drew a sellout crowd. The university had never seen this kind of press for the wrestling team. Even back then, people came to see Brock Lesnar.

Instead of just reporting about my wrestling career and maybe even how I might approach my next match, the media got to be really invasive. They asked too damn many questions.

One day, I decided I had enough. I told J I wasn't going to cooperate with the press anymore. I just wanted to wrestle. Except when I was out there competing, I wanted the press to leave me the hell alone. But instead of getting off my back, the media wanted to talk to me even more.

To this day, the media coverage is the one part of fame that I really don't enjoy. I love being in front of the audience, but I've always hated the "public relations" bullshit.

I try to limit media access and get some personal space, but when I do, it only makes them hungrier. They are like animals. If you feed them once, they always come back for another bite. And another. And another.

That's why I learned very early on not to give them the whole meal at once. They will always come back, and I have to save something to feed them when they do.

I went to summer school before my senior year at the university, but I also coached at J Robinson's wrestling camps to make a few bucks. I was about to start my senior year when word came down that there were now only ten scholarships available for wrestling. Ten scholarships meant that if the program wanted to add more wrestlers, it would have to divide full scholarships into partials, or that some wrestlers would be on their own. There just weren't enough scholarships to go around.

You guessed it. Next thing I know, I'm being told the university is cutting what little of a scholarship I had so they can give it to another guy. I was really pissed. I'm bringing in fans and dollars to the program, but after four years of working my ass off, I am stuck with a pile of student loans. That pissed me off almost as much as losing to Neal my junior year. The whole situation still chaps my ass.

I was on my own again. This time, though, I was a senior, and I knew it was my last chance.

I just said, "Screw it," and went undefeated until a week before the Big Ten tournament at the end of the season.

It was me against Wes Hand from the University of Iowa. Wes and I had wrestled a handful of times in my junior year, and he had me figured out. I shot in on him, and he lateral-dropped me right to my back. Fifteen seconds into the match I was down 5–0. In Division I wrestling, that means you're hosed.

I wasn't going down that way . . . not to him, not to anyone . . . I kept saying to myself, "You're Brock Lesnar, no one does this to you . . ." and I battled my way back. But he gets his dancing shoes on and just tries to stay away from me with his five-point lead. I ended up coming back and scoring four straight points, but there just wasn't enough time, and Wes Hand beat me 5–4.

I don't have to tell you that I was humiliated—again. I wasn't five years old anymore, but my mom still chewed me out. She was big on tough love, and I deserved the ass chewing.

When we went to Outback Steakhouse that night, I couldn't even finish my steak. I was sickened by the loss. I didn't have any excuse for losing. I thought to myself, "No one should be able to beat me. I am better than that. I am better than Wes Hand."

When I look back, though, that loss was the best thing that could have happened to me. It made me work harder than ever before, and it made me focus on the Big Ten tourney, which was the last important match before the NCAA Championships. Two weeks after my only loss, I won the Big Ten Championship by beating Wes Hand in the final, 2–1.

For both me and Wes Hand, however, the biggest match of our lives was still a week away. Sixty-four heavyweights . . . the best in the country . . . competing for the NCAA National Championship. If Hand and I could both get through our thirty-two-man brackets, we were going to wrestle each other for the title. I couldn't wait.

It was a long year since I had lost to Stephen Neal, and this was my last chance to become the NCAA Division I Heavyweight Champion. I wanted to win that title so bad. It was what I had gone through all this shit for. I came back all the way from defeat at the hands of Stephen Neal, and I was headed back into the finals. This was my chance for redemption, an opportunity to live my dream, a shot at attaining my goal.

I couldn't sleep the night before we left for the NCAA tournament. The Mississippi River runs through campus, and I walked down to this spot where we used to do training runs.

As I stood there by the river, I said to myself, "There isn't a man in the world that can stop me from standing on that podium as the NCAA Heavyweight Champion. Not Wes Hand, not anyone else they put in front of me. I'm coming home as the champion. That title is mine."

And then a sense of calm came over my body. I went home and slept like a baby. I got up the next day and we flew down to St. Louis, Missouri, for my final matches as a college wrestler.

Getting to the finals in my senior year was a bitch. I had lost in the finals the year before, and it was burning my ass every day. Plus, you know the old expression: "Everything that can go wrong, will!"

I went through my entire senior year with a knee injury. I also had to have a salivary gland surgically removed from my neck during the season. I wasn't the wrestler that I could have been, but I was determined to be good enough to become the NCAA Champion.

Sixty-four guys were invited to the NCAA tournament. After several matches sixty-two were done, and the stage was set. Brock Lesnar vs. Wes Hand for the third and final time. And let me tell you, it was a fuckin' nail-biter. We wrestled our asses off, and ended up with a tie. So the match goes into overtime. Still no winner.

When we got to the second overtime, I won the coin toss, which allowed me to choose to be on top or bottom. I knew I could ride Wes Hand, but I chose to go down. I wanted to explode out of there. Your best chance of getting away from your opponent is right off the whistle. It's the element of surprise. I tried to beat the whistle and Wes stopped me.

As our match continued, I went to stand up, but Wes pulled me down. I tried to switch, turned him around with a hip-heist, and escaped with nine seconds left. One point Lesnar. I did it. Everything I worked for . . . all the sacrifice . . . the dedication . . . the pain . . . the hopes and dreams of my family, who had sacrificed along with me . . . this was the moment we spent years fighting for. All that effort culminated in one brief moment when I was officially declared the NCAA Division I Heavyweight Wrestling Champion!

Two weeks before that, J Robinson had taught me the hip-heist. Great timing. Thanks, J.

I'M AN NCAA CHAMPION:
NOW WHAT?

AN OLD COLLEGE roommate of J Robinson's watched the NCAA tournament, and he wanted to meet me. His name was Gerry Brisco, and he worked for the company that was known back then as the World Wrestling Federation. They have since changed their name to World Wrestling Entertainment, or WWE, but in 2000 they were the WWF, and they were proud of their federation.

This is my book, and I'm calling them the WWE. If you don't like it, skip to the UFC chapters.

As my college days were winding down I really had to think about what I wanted to do with my life. A lot of people ask me why I didn't go for the 2000 Olympics in Sydney, Australia. The answer to that one is easy. I was sick and tired of being broke.

I knew guys who were chasing the Olympic dream. They were

driving up to the gym in their broken-down cars, working nine-to-five jobs to support their training. I had already been doing that my whole life. After everything I put myself through to win the NCAA title, I was done paying dues. It was time to cash in. My dream was never the Olympics. It was to win the NCAA Heavyweight Championship. I achieved my goal, and I knew in my heart it was time to move on.

The university was helping me in my transition from student athlete to professional. At the time, I was thinking about trying either professional football or professional wrestling. The school had a legal department, and they set up interviews for me with different attorneys and agents. I picked a Minneapolis lawyer named David Bradley Olsen, because he had the most experience. He had represented professional wrestlers, including Jesse "The Body" Ventura, and he had sued the WWE a couple of times.

I had also met NFL head coach Tony Dungy a few times because he played football for the University of Minnesota back in the day. He wanted me to try out for the NFL in Tampa Bay, where he was calling the shots. Tony had a lot of faith in my ability to make the team, but I made a big decision the night before I was going to get on the plane for Florida. The NFL was going to have to wait. I was being offered a sure thing, and was going to become a professional wrestler.

Again, it was really simple. WWE offered me guaranteed money, including a big signing bonus with no strings attached. I would even get paid a huge salary for the time I was training to be a pro wrestler.

My lawyers have told me I can't print how much I signed for, because of a confidentiality clause. Here's what I can say: I signed the biggest development deal in WWE history. I can also tell you that I had absolutely no idea how lucrative my contract was, because I didn't know anyone in the wrestling business. I hadn't even watched five minutes of pro wrestling in my life. All I knew was that I was a poor kid with student loans, and I was being offered more money than I'd ever seen in my entire life. Brock Lesnar was off to join the circus!

PART II

THE NEXT BIG THING

FAITH, FAMILY, FEDERATION

I **REMEMBER MY** first meeting with WWE. I was twenty-two years old, and Vince McMahon flew me and my lawyer out to Connecticut. As soon as we landed, there was a limousine waiting to take us to the WWE world headquarters in Stamford. The place was a little different from the gymnasiums I was used to, and looked like a rock concert that had collided with a wrestling museum. There were televisions everywhere showing WWE highlights. Heavy metal was playing over the sound system. Posters of "WWE Superstars" lined the walls. There was a state-of-the-art gym and weight room, a full-service cafeteria, and a television production studio. For a farm boy from South Dakota, it was all pretty impressive.

For those of you who don't know, Vince McMahon is world famous, and he is rich. Very rich. Since the 1980s, he has appeared on national television every week in his own programs, and he is the face of the WWE. But in addition to the "role" of WWE chairman he plays on TV, he is also the owner and creative mind behind the entire company. Vince is the absolute boss. Nothing happens in that company without his say-so. He is a big, bodybuilder type, with slick dark hair and a booming voice. He is larger than life, and can sell snow cones to Eskimos. But I wasn't a pro wrestling fan at the time, so when I walked in, all I saw was the guy who could sign my paycheck.

Vince was flanked by his lawyer, Ed Kaufman; Gerald Brisco; and Jim "J.R." Ross. Kaufman was a typical corporate type, and looked totally out of place. Brisco was a former amateur and professional wrestler who worked behind the scenes at the TV tapings, and also as a talent scout for the company. J.R. was the host of the TV shows, the play-by-play announcer who was also—at that time—the executive vice president of talent relations.

We all sat down at a large conference table in Vince's spacious office. I don't recall all of the details of the meeting, but there was one moment I'll never forget.

As Vince and his team were explaining what I could expect from life in the WWE (remember, it was still WWF, or World Wrestling FEDERATION, at the time), J.R. leaned over the table, looked me dead in the eye, and said with his Oklahoma drawl, "Mr. Lesnar, there are three things we take very seriously in this company: Faith, Family, and Federation." I didn't know what the hell he was talking about, so I just nodded.

I sure got it after a couple of years on the road, because by then I thought I'd lost my faith . . . I didn't have a family because I was on the road three hundred days a year . . . and all I had was the Federation. That's how Vince McMahon ends up owning all these guys. All they have is that company, that business. All they have is what Vince allows them to have. He owns their careers, and their careers become their lives, so he owns them.

It's a vicious cycle. These guys sacrifice and sacrifice and sacrifice. Then they make it, which means they have to work three hundred days a year, in a different city every night. That's when they lose their homes and their families. They end up working themselves to death, paying for homes they rarely visit, for kids they never see, and for ex-wives and then ex-wives' homes.

Even early on, I could see that is not how I wanted to end up. But I have to say, between that first meeting with Vince, and the last time I laced up my wrestling boots, it was one hell of a wild ride.

PRO WRESTLING 101

AS SOON AS Vince was sure I was serious about professional wrestling, and that I was willing to make the necessary commitment, we got down to business. In no time at all we agreed on the money, shook hands, and I was on my way.

My lawyer took care of the details, and just saying that now sounds funny to me. Only a few weeks before, I had gone to "my lawyer's" office in downtown Minneapolis for the first time, and I had to borrow money from him to get out of the parking ramp. Now I was paying him to look out for me.

Before the ink on my new contract was even dry, I was told that I had to relocate to Ohio Valley Wrestling (OVW), WWE's developmental territory in Louisville, Kentucky, to begin my pro wrestling training as soon as possible. I called J.R. and told him that I had some amateur wrestling community commitments in Minnesota, and it would be few weeks before I could make it to Louisville. I got lucky on that one, because WWE was working hard to develop a recruitment "understanding" with the amateur wrestling community, and I was given the extra time.

For the first time in my life, I had money in my pocket. I used my signing bonus to pay off my student loans, and I bought a motorcycle. I hadn't even stepped foot into a wrestling ring yet, and I was debt-free. Those WWE paychecks were coming in every week, and I thought I had it made.

I've heard people say I got a handout from WWE because I got a big contract without coming up through the ranks like everyone else. That just pisses me off. I've never asked for a handout in my life, and I'd never take one if offered. Vince McMahon didn't become a billionaire by giving money away. People who think I got a handout from the WWE, or from anyone else for that matter, have no idea what they're talking about.

Truth is, I worked my ass off to become an NCAA Division I Heavyweight Champion. Nobody handed me that honor. I worked for it. After I accomplished that goal, I looked at myself as a commodity, for sale to the highest bidder—similar to the dairy products we produced on the farm back in Webster. I knew I had a high value in the market because, after years of hard work, I was a rare commodity. I was a six-foot three-inch, 285-pound athletic freak of nature. I was built like a big man, but could move like a small man. On top of all that, I wasn't just some local college wrestling champion from half a decade earlier. The NCAA Heavyweight Champion is wrestling's equivalent of a Heisman Trophy winner, and I had just won the title.

During my college days, I proved that I had that certain something. Love me or hate me, people paid to watch me compete. Vince McMahon knew I could put asses in the seats. That is a rare talent, I took it to the market, and the market rewarded me.

Even though I was going to remain in Minnesota for a while, I still wanted to get a jump on my pro wrestling training. I never do anything half-ass. I wanted to learn from the best and it didn't take me long to learn that meant a call to Brad Rheingans.

Brad was a decorated amateur wrestler. He was an NCAA champion in 1975 for North Dakota State University, and placed fourth in the 1976 Olympics. He qualified for the Olympic team in 1980, but didn't compete due to the United States boycott. All that hard work, and he didn't get a chance to pursue the dream.

Brad had also been an active professional wrestler for over a decade. In the United States, he was best known for his work with Verne Gagne's American Wrestling Association (AWA). He also worked overseas for New Japan Pro Wrestling, first as a wrestler and later as an agent for the office.

Lots of the wrestlers who headlined big shows for many years have nothing to show for it, but Brad was smart and saved his money. All of it. I bet that cheap-ass has the first dollar he ever made. And now, because he worked so hard to save, he has a great life. Brad has a beautiful home, and can go hunting and fishing whenever he feels like it. He enjoys his time, and he should. He earned everything he has, and his body bears the scars of years on the mat and in the ring.

Soon after I started with Brad, I realized he was doing me a special favor. First, I found out that Brad had had stopped running camps for aspiring pro wrestlers over a year before he agreed to bring me in. Then, about two or three weeks into my training camp, I went out to lunch with Dan Jesser. Dan was a local wrestler that wanted to make it big-time, and at the time, he was one of the top guys on the independent circuit in Minnesota.

We were just shooting the shit, and I mentioned that I had talked to Brad about something at Brad's house. Dan looked at me in shock and said, "Brad doesn't let anybody in his house!" Dan told me had been working with Brad for eight years and had never once been invited over.

From that day on, I knew Brad considered me to be more than just a student. We were developing a long-standing relationship and building a true friendship. Brad trained hundreds of students over the years, and training those guys was always just business; but with me, it was different. Brad became my older brother, and to this day, he's family. Brad doesn't have a large family—it's just him, his mom, and her husband, Jim. At Christmastime, Thanksgiving, all the family holidays, Brad is always welcome at our dinner table. I've opened my home to him the same way he opened his home to me.

CURT HENNIG

WHILE I WAS training with Brad, I met someone who would become another great influence in my pro wrestling career. His name was Curt Hennig, and I wish he was here today to read this chapter.

Curt was a second-generation wrestler, the son of a big time wrestler in the AWA territory named Larry "The Axe" Hennig. When the old timers all get together and start shooting the shit about "the good old days" of the AWA, they all talk about what a big tough son of a bitch Larry Hennig was in his prime. Curt's dad smartened him up early about what the pro wrestling business had to offer, and the price you have to pay to achieve success in it.

Curt taught me something that sticks with me to this day—in the wrestling business, you have to "Get in to get out!"

I can still hear him say the line. Curt knew the pro wrestling business was built on a pile of people who had been used for everything they were worth, and then dumped on the side of the road. I'm not saying that's right or wrong. I'm just saying that's how it is. Since that's the score in pro wrestling, Curt came up with the idea that the only way to keep your sanity, or your health, was to "get in to get out."

I wish he practiced what he preached. Curt got in and really got out. He died in 2003. Nice rib . . .

I really think about him every day. We could have had so much fun together. I miss him so much, because with Curt you were never just passing time. You were enjoying every minute of it.

Why did he have to go and die?

LOUISVILLE

AFTER TRAINING WITH Brad for only a few months and fulfilling my commitments to the amateur wrestling community, I was ready to head to Louisville and enter the WWE developmental system. I had started to watch a little pro wrestling on TV so I could see what I was getting myself into. I bought a pickup truck, loaded all my things into the back, and hit the road.

When I arrived in Louisville, I met up with former Golden Gopher Shelton Benjamin. I followed him as the number one heavyweight at the university, and he stayed on as an assistant coach while I was there. Like me, Shelton had signed with WWE after being recruited by Gerald Brisco. Shelton and I found a two-bedroom apartment to rent, and I was ready to start training.

My first training session was at nine o'clock on a Monday morning. When I got there, I couldn't believe it. The "OVW training center" was nothing more than a little box in the middle of a warehouse district. I thought, "I'm working for this huge international company, and this is where all the big-time television wrestlers get trained?"

When I walked in the door, Danny Davis came right up to meet me. Danny was the owner of OVW and also the head trainer. I liked Danny from the beginning, and we became pretty good friends when I was in Louisville. I have nothing but good things to say about Danny.

On my first day, he asked me, "Can you hit the ropes, kid?" There I was, NCAA Heavyweight Champion, almost three hundred pounds, ready to take on the world, and Danny wanted to know if I could hit the ropes. I thought to myself, "I've done this thousands of times at Brad's—I'll show this SOB just how hard and fast I can come off the ropes, and how good I look doing it."

I got in the ring and, with a full head of steam, threw myself into the ring ropes just like I did every day back at Brad's camp. But instead of launching my body back across the ring like I was supposed to, I went straight through the ropes and crash-landed on the concrete floor with everyone watching. I nearly broke my ass in the process.

What I didn't know at the time is that there are different types of "ropes" for wrestling rings. When I trained in Minnesota, Brad had an old-style WCW wrestling ring, with ropes made from steel cable covered by a garden hose with tape over it. Danny's ropes were made out of real rope (just like the WWE used). Real rope has a lot more give to it than cable. I learned that the hard way.

Looking back, I can see that making a fool out of myself was a good icebreaker, because it showed everyone I was human—I make mistakes and bleed like everybody else. I can laugh about it now, but it wasn't the least bit funny to me then.

Despite my initial stumble, I progressed quickly and excelled in practice every day. I understood what they were teaching, and I could do the things they wanted me to do in the ring.

In a matter of weeks, Danny Davis decided to put me and Shelton together as a team, and we started going to all the little towns in the area, wrestling in front of tiny crowds in bingo halls, local community churches, high school gyms, you name it. We were working with a number of guys who are pretty well known today, but at the time were just starting out like I was: Batista, John Cena, Randy Orton, Mark Henry.

It was a pretty easy life at OVW compared to the training I was used to. We were home every night, and the checks came in steady, without fail.

Danny gave me the "honor" of transporting the ring to each show, and then back to his house for storage. He said he chose me because I kept talking about my work ethic, but I think it had more to do with the fact that I had a pickup truck. Regardless, the ring was my responsibility.

Since I was in charge of the ring, I made sure all the other guys were there on time to help set it up. If they weren't, Danny heard about it, because to me it was a team effort. I didn't give a shit how long somebody had been there. And nobody was going to give me any back talk either, because if they did, they were going to have to get into it with me. I don't think I was disliked for making everyone carry their own weight, but if I was, I really didn't give a damn.

I was there to excel, and I had made up my mind to be better than anyone I was training with. I wasn't at OVW to win a popularity contest. I was there to learn so I could move up to the WWE where the big money was.

Some guys at OVW would stay out late every night so they could act like they were somebody for the locals in the bar. I probably ended up at the bar only twice a month, at the most, because I had no desire or interest in trying to impress the locals down there. I wanted to hit the gym in the morning before practice, do my workouts in the ring, and then have the rest of the day off. At the time, we were only doing the local wrestling shows three nights a week, with weekends off, so I had a lot of time to myself—just the way I like it.

I had a good time at OVW. Danny and his wife, Julie, were great to me. Just like with Brad, my relationship with Danny was more than just teacher–student. We actually became friends.

Danny invited me into his home, and I appreciated it. I was at Danny's house often (because the ring was there), and Danny and Julie would usually invite me in for lunch. In exchange for the free lunches, I did some handyman work for them here and there. That's one thing about being a farm boy: you learn to fix anything. But I also knew that if I offered to fix something, Danny would always cook me a big steak when I was done. We remain friends to this day.

After a while, I knew I had learned all I was going to learn in Louisville. John Laurinaitis was just then transitioning into the role of WWE's VP of talent relations, and I told him I was done doing the small local shows, and that I needed a bigger challenge. I told John, "If you want me to get better, then you need to put me in the ring with better people!"

I asked John to give me a chance at the next level—just a couple of "dark matches" to show them how far along I had come. The dark matches are non-televised matches done right before television tapings to warm up the crowd and to let the WWE brass take a look at you.

I knew all I needed was a chance. Let me perform on the non-televised portion of the show, I told John, and I will work harder and better than everyone else. If I can show you what I've got, I'll be up on the main roster.

If I didn't belong, I knew Vince would get rid of me. He was paying me too much to wait forever for me to make him a return on his investment. But as far as I was concerned, I had done my time in the Louisville minor leagues, and it was time for me to see how far I could go in the big time. I reminded John that both J.R. and Brisco had said I would only be in Louisville for a year, and by that point I had been in Louisville for a year and four months. I felt like someone had lied to me. I had done my time. I was headed back home to Minneapolis.

THE NEXT BIG THING

WITHIN DAYS OF RETURNING to Minneapolis, I received the call. WWE wanted me to go on the road with them, and start out by doing dark matches. The fight to make it as a wrestling entertainer was on.

The very first dark matches I remember are the ones where they put me in the ring with Billy Gunn. We were in Nashville or Knoxville (all these towns ended up being the same to me real quick) one night, and Curt and Brad had come down to watch. I was doing the Shooting Star Press—an inward backflip off the top rope to a full layout landing on top of my opponent—at the time, and both Curt and Brad had these looks on their faces like, "What the hell is wrong with you, Brock?"

They both got on me right away, saying "You're gonna have a

pretty short career if you keep doing that three-hundred-pound gorilla backflip. Figure out a new finish."

Those guys told me straight up, because they cared. "Leave that to the smaller guys," Curt said. "They need every advantage they can grab in this business. You don't need that move. It's not worth the risk." But I kept doing the Shooting Star, because it was spectacular. I wanted to be the best, and no one my size should be able to pull off that move.

If you can't picture the sight of a three-hundred-pound man rotating through the air and crashing down on his opponent, or if you've never seen me do the Shooting Star, the videos are easy to find on the Internet. You will be amazed by what you see. You will also be horrified when you see what happens when I don't land the move. I'm lucky that I didn't end up in a wheelchair.

In the beginning, I was traveling with Kurt Angle and Taz. That was both good and bad, because both of those guys played pretty big roles in my development, and my near destruction.

Kurt Angle was the 1996 Olympic Gold Medal winner in wrestling, and I liked the way he approached the wresting entertainment business, because when he laced up his boots, the shit was on. The word on Kurt was that he only had one gear, and that was hyper-overdrive.

Kurt and I got to know each other pretty well because we had amateur wrestling in common. And he answered my questions about the business of pro wrestling because he started a few years before me.

Kurt could have turned to ultimate fighting right after the 1996 Olympics, but the timing would've been bad. The UFC wasn't "happening" in 1996, and the money was nothing like it is today.

The very first day I met Brad Rheingans, he told me, "Life is about timing." It didn't dawn on me at that moment, but years later I got it. Everything has to fall into the right time frame. If you're not in the right place at the right time, it's not going to happen for you.

To this day I get asked questions about Kurt and his chances as an MMA fighter. Let's get one thing straight: Kurt Angle was one tough son of a bitch. Could Kurt in his prime have fought in the UFC? Absolutely. And he would have torn it up. Could Kurt fight in UFC now? Absolutely not. After all of his pro wrestling injuries, I don't think he could even pass the physical.

Taz was a unique guy, too. Here was this sawed-off, pissed-off wrestler whose biggest push was behind him, and he was trying his hardest to transition into the role of an on-air commentator. Why not? It's a great gig, the money is good, and you don't have to take bumps in the ring every night.

Taz could talk his ass off, which would have made him a good commentator, and did make him an entertaining guy to be in the car with. Taz was also a big amateur wrestling fan, knew my history, and he knew I wanted to make it to the top. I wasn't shy about it, and he liked that about me.

One day Taz heard the stupid way they wanted me to work in a dark match—old-fashioned, plodding, monster heel, fake pro wrestling bullshit. Taz just shook his head. He said, "That sucks." No sugarcoating, no bullshit. I liked that about Taz. He had been around for a long time, and he wasn't playing the corporate puppet. He respected my credentials, and I respected his honesty. Taz heard all these veterans giving me bad advice about how a big man is supposed to work, but I knew it was a new day and age. Taz knew it too, so he took me over to meet Paul Heyman.

As you know, Paul is writing this book with me, so it's kind of funny talking about him, but this is where we became instant friends. I didn't know Paul from Adam, but he got involved in my next two dark matches. Paul went right to Vince McMahon and went to bat for me.

All of a sudden the machine started getting ready for me. I was told I was needed at *WrestleMania* in Toronto, and I'd be wrestling during the Fan Axxess convention. Next thing I know, Paul is pulling me aside, all excited, and says, "We're starting on TV the day after *Mania*."

I made my national TV debut in March 2002. I started by doing these run-ins, which are brief appearances on camera, where I would jump in the ring and hit people with my finishing maneuver, which they ended up calling the "F-5." The maneuver consisted of me throwing my opponent up over my head, spinning him, then slamming him to the canvas all in one fluid motion. Everyone ate it up. WWE fans were looking for a new star, and here I was just smashing everything in my path.

After my first TV shot, everything happened so fast. It's really all just a blur. Kind of like I've been F-5'd myself.

My entire time in WWE was a blur, actually, but those first few months were even blurrier. Paul became my on-air "agent," (they didn't want him to be an old-school "wrestling manager," and Vince liked the idea of a heel agent because he hated dealing with Hollywood agents), and I got moved into a program pretty quick with the Hardy Boyz. I really liked working with them. They could move around, the crowds loved them, and they could sell my moves in a way that got the audience into the match and mad at me. Lita, one of the WWE "divas," was dating Matt Hardy at the time, and she was with them on camera as well, so that gave me and Paul someone else to pick on to get even more heat. Nothing like picking on a woman to get a crowd riled up.

I want to mention something here in this book quickly, and then I want to move on from the subject:

While all this is happening, my daughter, Mya, was born. Right after my debut, and just as I started going on the road, this little baby came into my life and changed everything forever. I became a father on April 10, 2002. No matter what I do for the rest of my life, I'll always be Mya Lynn

Lesnar's father first and foremost. I love Mya very much, and I can tell you that from the day my daughter was born, I have been a blessed man because of her.

I was picking up some really good steam on television, and I started getting booked for WWE shows all over the world right away. In the business, the more you work, and the more fans you draw, the more you make. While my paychecks were getting bigger and bigger, I was away from home more and more. That's the trade-off, and it's just another way the wrestling business eats you up.

Life on the road was wild. I was flying to a new city every day, and living the life of a rock star. Everywhere I went people knew me. I was having a great time, and who wouldn't? Money. Girls. More girls. More money.

The only problem was that none of it was real. It wasn't a life. It was killing time. I would look around the locker room before shows and think how lucky I was. I was probably the youngest guy there, and I was headed straight to the top. The other guys in that room weren't so lucky. They were trapped in the life. They had no way out. They were drinking and popping pain pills like they were going out of style, and they were miserable because they had lost their faith along with their families—all they had was the Federation.

I didn't want to be an old man, pulling pads over my surgically repaired, broken-down knees, struggling to pull on my elbow pads with arthritic shoulders, popping pain pills to make it through one more big-money match. So as much fun as I was having, even right off the bat I was thinking about how I was going to get out. Curt's words were ringing in my ears: "Get in to get out."

Once we got past the Hardys, the rocket ship was really strapped to my ass, and the fuse was lit. That's when the whole deal went down involving the match that never happened with Stone Cold Steve Austin, one of the WWE's biggest stars at the time. Why was he a star? "Because Stone Cold says so." He was a big, tough, raunchy, rude, crude, beer-guzzling good ol' boy, and the crowds couldn't get enough of him.

Paul knows the story better than I do, because he was behind the scenes with Vince, and I was just doing my job, being on time, wrestling my matches, collecting my paychecks. But I'll do my best to tell you what I remember.

I got to Atlanta, and the WWE road agent told me I would be working with Steve that night, and that I was going to beat him somehow. But minutes later, everything changed. I heard that Steve had walked out. Went home. With Steve gone, Vince needed to do something quick.

Paul pulled me aside and brought me two steaks from Vince's office. He always stole a couple of Vince's afternoon steaks and brought them to me. I never asked if Vince knew. I was just happy to get the prime cut.

As I worked on the steak, Paul explained the new swerve: Vince himself was going to wrestle Ric Flair that night, in Atlanta—a battle between two fiftysomething guys—with the story-line being a winner-take-all bet for Vince's story-line 50 percent of WWE ownership against Flair's story-line 50 percent. But just when it looked to the crowd like Flair was going to beat Vince, I'd come down, jump into the ring, and cost Flair the match. Vince would then owe a huge favor to the Next Big Thing.

According to our quickly prepared script, Paul was supposed to call in my favor for me by telling Vince, on national TV, that if I won at *King of the Ring 2002*, I would get a title shot at the *SummerSlam* pay-per-view. The fans watching the show didn't know it yet, but Vince had already decided to make me the youngest WWE Heavyweight Champion in history.

Here I was, just a few months after my official TV debut, and only a year out of college, and I was being set up to take the WWE title in the main event of the second biggest pay-per-view of the year.

I had been watching my checks get bigger and bigger every week, and I couldn't even imagine how much I was about to make from those two events. The main event of a pay-per-view show is as big as it gets in our business.

That's just it. It was always about business for me. I wasn't in it for the fame or the glory, though I had some fun with both for a little while. I was in it for the money. I wanted to feed my family, give my parents and my children the best lives that I could provide for them, and get out while I was still relatively young and healthy.

That summer on my rocket ship to the top just flew by. I don't really remember making my Madison Square Garden debut against Ric Flair, but I sure remember getting paid for it. I don't remember how many times we went to the UK that summer, but I remember that my paycheck got bigger each and every time I went back. I don't remember any specifics about the *King of the Ring* pay-per-view, but I remember it being by far the biggest payday I had to that point in my career.

That's what happens when you live on the road, and in front of the TV cameras. You can't tell one town from the other, or one show from the next. They all just blend together. You get up in a hotel that looks like all of the other hotels, drive to the airport in a generic rental car, get on a plane, and don't care where you land . . . because it's always the same. The routine gets old really fast, and it never changes.

Sometimes I'd get lucky enough to get into the town early enough so I go could go to a gym, and maybe find a decent meal. After that, though, it would be just killing time until I had to go to the arena. I couldn't really do much, because fans recognized me everywhere I went. So, most often, I just stayed in my room.

Once I got to the arena, I had to shake everyone's hand. Because that's the unwritten law. As if God himself made it the 11th commandment. I hadn't seen the boys since we all stood around the baggage claim at the airport a few hours before, hoping our bags would come around quickly so we could beat everyone else to the rental car line. But we would always shake hands, and everyone would smile like they were glad to see each other. It was all so insincere and phony it made me sick.

Meanwhile, while I'm going through the motions on the never-ending treadmill that road life had become, all I could think of was getting home so I could see my baby daughter Mya, because she would grow up just a little bit more every day I was gone. I was missing out on all these wonderful experiences with my child, missing out on all the greatest things about being a dad, and was doing the bullshit "shaking-hands routine" with a bunch of people I just saw a few hours ago like they were long-lost brothers. It was insane.

It got to the point that I remember one day looking across the locker room at Ric Flair, who was then in his midfifties, and saying to myself, "That's not going to be me." I don't mean that as any disrespect toward Ric. He gave his life to the wrestling business. He was truly one of the greats, and he deserves a lot of credit for what he did.

But with all the greatness that his name is supposed to represent, and all the years he had spent on top, what the hell was he still doing there? He got in, but he never got out.

I wasn't going to be the guy missing his kids' birthday parties and graduations.

I wondered how many of his own kids' birthday parties did Flair miss? How many of their graduations? I didn't want to be pushing sixty years old and still wearing tights.

Flair was known as the best, and if the business could break him, it could happen to anyone. Even me. That's why, every time I looked at Flair, every time I saw him climb in the ring and let out his trademark "Woooooooooooooooo!," I heard Curt Hennig's voice in my head: "Get in to get out."

WINNING THE TITLE...
FROM THE ROCK

I ONLY WRESTLED Dwayne "The Rock" Johnson three times. The first time was in Australia, right before we worked the *SummerSlam* main event at the Nassau Coliseum in Long Island, New York, for the Undisputed WWE Championship. I had won the *King of the Ring* and was headed for my first pay-per-view main event. There's a lot of pressure on someone when they have to main-event with the top star of the day. You have to be careful not to hurt the Golden Goose, but you also have to make your match look good.

To get me ready for the Rock, we did a match on television against Hulk Hogan. This was a big deal, because Hogan didn't wrestle every week on TV. WWE was portraying him as the legend of all legends, and to make me the focal point of the promotion, we were going to do a major incident on television where I took Hulk Hogan OUT. I was honored to get into the ring with Hogan, but at the same time, I looked at things a little differently from everyone else. Yes, Hogan was the biggest star of the eighties and nineties. He drew huge gates and sold millions of pay-per-views. This guy had made more money than any other wrestler of his era, but here he was, squeezing out another run at age fiftysomething . . . just like Ric Flair.

So we did this deal with Hulk Hogan where I took Hogan out violently on the WWE *Smackdown!* TV show. I knew the script, because Paul was the lead writer of the show, and we communicated all the time. Vince kept telling me we needed to make this as memorable a night as possible for the fans, because this was a big moment in my career. I was going to slay the immortal Hulk Hogan, bust him open, and leave him for dead. Other wrestlers had "jumped" Hogan from behind before, or "attacked" him to build interest in an upcoming match, but I was going to beat the crap out of him face-to-face. Vince didn't just want me to "get over," he wanted me over the top. There was a lot riding on that *SummerSlam* pay-per-view, and WWE was counting on a big buy rate to carry the promotion into the fall.

The Rock was a proven commodity, but putting a rookie in the main event of your second biggest show of the year was a risk. Vince liked to take chances in life, but he called them "calculated risks." The idea was to really pump up the interest in my match with The Rock by having me hit Hulk Hogan with the F-5, crack him over the head with a chair, bust his head open, and wipe his blood across my chest like Brock The Conqueror. It was pretty dramatic stuff. Vince figured if that didn't position me as a top star with the WWE audience, and give me the boost and credibility needed to draw some serious money with the Rock at *SummerSlam*, nothing would.

Behind the scenes, Hogan was being written out of the future scripts, and he wasn't going to appear at the Australia show. With no Hogan to work the main event Down Under, it gave me and Dwayne a chance to work with each other for the first time, and to feel each other out before we got in the ring with everyone watching at *SummerSlam*. We were in Melbourne doing a Triple Threat Match (three wrestlers in the ring at the same time), with the Rock defending his Undisputed WWE Heavyweight Championship against both me and HHH.

When Dwayne and I got in the ring together, we could both tell that we had instant chemistry. I know we stole the show. Everyone could immediately tell we were going to be big box office against each other. It was a week and a half before *SummerSlam*, and we were ready.

WWE needed a new champion, because Dwayne was taking time off after the show to do a movie, so the key here was to go all the way with this kid, Brock Lesnar, because I had to carry the load for the company while Dwayne was off shooting films. Not everyone has what it takes to sell tickets on a nightly basis at major arenas, and sell millions of dollars' worth of pay-per-views several times a year. That's what a champion does. Vince thought I had what it took to pull that off.

Dwayne, of course, is a very smart guy. He was going to have his character, the Rock, do a clean job for me because he wanted to grease the wheels for himself to come back when the time was right. Dwayne knew putting me over was right for business, and he was willing to take a loss for the team, on pay-per-view, in front of all of his fans. He saw the talent I had, and he knew it would be best for the company if there were no questions in the fans' minds that I beat him "fair and square." That way, after I had my ride at the top, he could beat me in a revenge match when he came back and he would look even better. It would be huge. WWE would make a lot of money. I'd make a lot of money. Dwayne would make a lot of money. That's the pro wrestling business at its best!

Dwayne also knew that it wasn't only right for business to put me over clean, but that Vince had it in his own head that the Rock should lose clean to Brock Lesnar. If Dwayne wanted the door open for a return, he had to keep Vince happy, and have him think that "Dwayne always gave back to the company, looked after what was right for business." Vince has ended more than one career when someone crossed him and put their own interests above the company's. Dwayne was too smart for that, and he did everything the right way . . . the smart way.

I don't know how many other guys Dwayne would have been happy to lose to clean, but he did it for me because he knew I could carry the torch for the company until he got it back. It wasn't a gift. It was business.

On August 25, 2002, at age twenty-five, I became the youngest WWE Champion in history when I "defeated" the Rock for the title at *SummerSlam*.

That night changed my life forever. I was now in a position to regularly score big paydays for a night's work, and more. I was now able to buy a lot of things. I'll always appreciate what Dwayne did for me and my family. If he hadn't made me look good, things might have been a lot different.

Beating the Rock at *SummerSlam 2002* made me a true superstar in the eyes of the fans. I didn't have just any title, I had the ultimate prize in sports entertainment, the Undisputed WWE Heavyweight Championship of the World. I wasn't just another guy in the locker room, or a curtain-jerker, or a midcard guy, or a guy hoping and praying to catch a break. I was the main event. People paid to see me. And that's exactly what I wanted, because that's where the serious money kicks in.

In my first-ever pay-per-view in some city I can't remember, I beat Jeff Hardy in an undercard match and got what I thought at the time was a decent check. Now I was headlining pay-per-views, and making life-changing money every time. Not a bad night's work. And it all literally happened overnight. Ten minutes in the ring with Jeff

Hardy was really cool. But twenty minutes in the ring with Dwayne, and I was set for life.

That's why the match with Dwayne was such a big moment in my life. It wasn't about who was better, who would really win. Come on, that's ridiculous. It was about the fact I wanted to buy my mom and dad a house. I wanted to put money away for my daughter's education. I wanted to be able to afford nice things in life for me and my family. I was the undisputed WWE Champion, on the fast track to fame and fortune. I was on top of the world.

And I was already looking over my shoulder, because I knew that the clock was ticking and my days were numbered.

THE UNDERTAKER

A S SOON AS I became Undisputed WWE Champion, the decision was made to let both *Raw* and *SmackDown!* have their own champions. So WWE branded two weekly shows that aired on different nights, and each brand carried its own roster of wrestlers.

My very first television appearance as the WWE Champion was on a *Monday Night Raw* that was broadcast live from Madison Square Garden. I know all these famous arenas mean something to a lot of people, and there is a lot of history in the Garden, but none of that means shit to me. Today, I like fighting in Las Vegas, because I have a routine there that I'm used to. Minnesota is great because I can just drive home that night. Anywhere else is just another place to me—just another in a long line of arenas in cities I don't get to see, with the same locker rooms where I have to shake everyone's hand, and then say good night and safe travels before meeting up with all of them in a few hours in a new city I won't get to see.

At the end of that first night on TV as champion, Paul and I jumped ship and went over to the *SmackDown!* roster—all part of the script, of course, as everything is in professional wrestling—and *Raw* was left without a champion. With Paul writing *SmackDown!*, I saw how this was going to play out. When I left *Raw*, it opened the door for HHH (who is now Vince's son-in-law) to be a champion. But that never bothered me. I really didn't care, because as long as I could just keep main-eventing the pay-per-views, things would be fine. HHH would be the World Champion on *Raw*. Good for him. I would be the WWE Champion on *SmackDown!* When it came time for the pay-per-views, someone had to be the top dog. Sometimes, that depended on the person you were defending the title against.

Advantage: Lesnar.

Why? Because my first feud as champion was against one of Vince's favorites, the Undertaker.

I have to say, there were some guys I liked wrestling with, or I guess I should say "performing" with. In the business, we just say "working," and I enjoyed working with the Big Show. I also liked working with Kurt Angle, Hulk Hogan, and Dwayne Johnson. I liked working with anyone who was what they called "over," which meant the person meant something to the audience. I liked working with anyone who was going to have some box-office appeal, because I was in the business to make money. The fame and the glory goes away. The money can help you and your family afford a better life.

Of all of the guys I worked with, I probably liked working with the Undertaker more than anyone else. Despite our personal differences, working with him was just so easy. He had that "Dead Man" gimmick, and he knew how to play it. Taker is a bright guy, too, and he knew I could make him look great. He also knew it was going to look believable when I beat him down.

Another reason I liked working with Taker is that it was so much easier for me to bump around the ring for his moves. He was a lot bigger than I was, and the fans not only loved his character, but they believed he was a legitimate badass. Bumping for a guy bigger than me is always going to be easier than bumping around all night long for the Hardy Boyz. It's just a different-style match. With the Hardys, you have to build and build and build until it's time to take that bump. With Taker, he's so big, you can just bump around right away.

There was also that mystique the Undertaker had. He was going to be the first person to really hand Brock Lesnar an ass kicking, so he was going to make it look good. I had no problem with that. As long as people were going to pay to see us go at it, I was happy.

We had our first pay-per-view match in Los Angeles, at the show called *Unforgiven*. Vince wanted us to do this finish where Taker ends up throwing me through a big set of lights at the top of the stage. I didn't like it, but I knew we were setting up the rematch, which would be a Hell-in-a-Cell match. That meant my first two pay-per-views as champion would be in the main-event position, which meant I was getting top pay.

That Hell-in-a-Cell match against The Undertaker was my favorite match in WWE. That night, everything just clicked the right way. Taker was on his game, and I was ready to go. People were convinced The Undertaker was either going to beat Brock Lesnar, or get his own ass beat pretty good. This wouldn't be just another monthly pay-per-view main event. This was going to be something special.

And it was.

NEXT IN LINE?
THE BIG SHOW!

MY NEXT OPPONENT after Undertaker was originally supposed to be Hulk Hogan. He was going to come back, looking for revenge after I hammered him on TV. Vince wanted to do a story line where Hogan was looking to settle the score, and the Lesnar vs. Hogan match would air live from Madison Square Garden as the main event of *Survivor Series 2002*. I would be headlining yet another pay-per-view. Vince wanted Hogan to look really good, but fall short of beating me for the title. I guess the ol' Hulkster didn't like that idea too much, and next thing I know, we were going with "Plan B" . . . the Big Show!

I had met Show when I was still in Louisville, and we didn't exactly hit it off right away. He pissed Vince or someone off because he was not in shape, and they sent him down to the developmental squad as a punishment. He was a giant of a man, seven feet tall and five-hundred-plus pounds, but Vince wanted his wrestlers to "look good." No one pays to see a couple of fat guys roll around the mat.

So I first met Show when I was in Louisville to learn the business, and I was taking everything seriously. I wanted to get called up to the main roster and the bigger paydays as soon as I could. When Show got demoted to Louisville, he looked at the guys training there like everyone was a maggot or something. He was all grumpy right from the get-go because he had to lose some weight, and everyone in camp was afraid of him. Everyone but me.

I wasn't afraid of Show, even if he did have almost a foot and two-hundred-some pounds on me, and I let him know it one day. We were in practice, and we got into the ring. He thought I was just another dumb jock greenhorn who was going to be intimidated by him, but I dropped him to the mat with a double leg takedown, and he was crying uncle. I kept the pressure on him because I didn't like the way he thought he was so much better than all the guys down there. I earned his respect that day, and I had no problem doing it either.

Another day, he was bullying everyone around, and I decided to bully him back. He got mad at me and told me, "I'll be back up in the main events, making millions, and you'll still be down here in Louisville setting up the ring."

When I got to the big time, I decided to remind Show of our little incidents in Louisville. As soon as I had to work with Show, I waited until the time was right and I said, "Remember down in Louisville, when you said—"

He cut me right off there and said, "I know where you are going with this, and fuck you!"

I still tortured the big bastard . . . and while I was doing it, I taunted him a little more. "Hey, didn't I take you down in front of everyone, too?" I laughed. But I like Show, because he turned out to be one of the best people you could ever be around.

Hell, he cried when I told everyone I was going to leave WWE. He's just a super nice, sentimental guy, and he's trapped in that massive body. That can't be easy. I know when I was three hundred pounds of muscle, it was hard to carry all that weight around. Imagine adding two hundred pounds of not-so-lean mass on top of that, and nine or ten more inches in height?

I loved working with Show because, just like with Undertaker, I'm in there with someone even I would call a monster. A lot of people consider me to be a monster, but Big Show really is one, so I didn't mind bumping my ass off for him. The difference in working with Taker and working with Show, besides that mystique Undertaker had, is that Show legitimately weighed five hundred pounds. That wasn't just a made up gimmick. He weighed five hundred pounds! Picking him up was a bitch. It hurt.

As big as he was, and as much as it hurt to pick his big ass up off the canvas and toss him, I had to do it, and I had to shine when I did, because WWE was planning to have Show beat me for the title. The story would have Paul "double-cross me," and help Big Show win the championship from the unbeaten Brock Lesnar. So, to set it up, I had to throw this five-hundred-pounder around every night, and that took a toll on my body fast.

The match at *Survivor Series* was very simple. I F-5'd Show, but Paul would then reveal that he "sold out Brock Lesnar" by breaking up the referee's count. About a minute later, I would get screwed out of the title. I was the biggest "heel," or "bad guy," in WWE, and I had just been robbed. The fans knew my character was going to go after Show and Paul for "revenge," which made me a new "babyface," or hero. I can't say my character became a "good guy," I was just going to beat up the guys people were willing to pay to see me pound on.

One night in South Africa, Show and I were working in the main event. We had been working with each other for months, and had come up with a pretty easy match we could do every night and make the people happy they had paid their money to see us. He'd go out to the ring with Paul, and Paul would cut a promo, getting the crowd all riled up, which wrestling people called "getting up the heat." Then I would come in, and we'd start the match hot, with me dumping the big bastard on his head a bunch of times. Show would get his heat, miss something, I'd smash him, F-5 him, and then F-5 Paul after the match. The fans loved it. I loved it, because we knew the routine, and it worked. No problems, right?

There we were in some city in South Africa. Think about it. South fuckin' Africa. Keep it simple. Same routine. It was safe, it worked, and I was hurting enough just throwing this five-hundred-pound monster around every night. I was tired . . . I was injured . . . and I didn't want any surprises.

Right before our match, Show came over to where I was dressing, smoking a cigarette. That alone is funny, because a cigarette in that huge hand looks like a cutoff toothpick. I hate cigarettes, and he had to know that. After I made him put the damn thing out, he said, "Let's change the match around tonight."

We're as far away from home as we can be. We might as well be on the planet Mars. We knew the match. It was easy. Why change it? Show got all upset with me, and he kept saying over and over again, "I'm a veteran, I'm the heel, I get to call the match!"

I couldn't believe he was serious. OK, we were all dealing with the stress from traveling halfway around the world. Bad news for Show, though. I wasn't in the mood for his shit that night.

"Whatever you wanna do is fine with me," I told the big grump, "just call it out in the ring."

So here's this seven-foot-tall, five-hundred-pound giant, and he's mumbling to himself as he walks away from me. It's so funny when I think about it now, because Show is the most likeable guy you'll ever meet, but he had me ready to kick his ass over in, of all places, South Africa!

Show was all huffy and puffy going out the ring, determined to call the match the way he wanted it to go, but as soon as I hit the ring, I snatched him and started suplexing him all over the place. Show backed me into a corner, and was going for a big chop across my chest, but I ducked under and waist-locked him. Once my hands were clasped, he had a pretty good idea about what was coming next. I was going to pivot my hips and throw him anywhere I wanted him to go. Show started screaming at me, "No no no no no no no no no," but I didn't listen. I threw him across the ring, and I can still hear the thud he made when he landed!

Before he could get up, I ran across the ring, grabbed him, and locked my hands around him again. He started panicking: "Brock, what the hell are you doing? Wait wait wait wait wait wait wait!" So I flung him around a few more times. He learned his lesson.

After that, we got along great. I flew around for Show when it came time for the part of the match they call "the heat," which is when the heel is getting the crowd angry by beating up the babyface, and building the anticipation for the babyface to get back up and kick the heel's ass. Show got on my nerves a little bit sometimes, but I could never hate him. I'm sure I got on his nerves, too, especially when I brought along a midget to dinner one night. By the way, Big Show fears midgets. I don't know why. It's a phobia. So just to "get" him, I brought one along . . . who kept sneaking bites out of Big Show's hamburger!

VODKA AND VICODINS

AS MY FIRST *WrestleMania* was approaching, I was already feeling the toll of life on the road and in the spotlight. I was hurt, dating back even before I dropped the title to the Big Show. My ribs were broken, and they hurt like hell, and I had a torn PCL (posterior crutiate ligament) in my right knee. I was flying to a new city every night, drinking more and more vodka and washing down more Vicodins, all just to dull the pain. It got old real fast. I kept thinking to myself that I was living a life that my mom and dad wouldn't want me living, and there was good reason for that.

It's easy for people to blame the wrestling business when top notch people like me get consumed, but that's just a cop-out. It's not the wrestling business' fault.

I could easily have ended up like some of the less fortunate. I had been popping pills for a while just to kill the pain of being on the road, of injuries that never heal, and I started drinking vodka. Lots of vodka. I can't even tell you how much for sure, but it seems like a bottle every one or two days, with a couple hundred pain pills each month to go with it. You want to know why there aren't more stories in this book about my pro wrestling days? Because the truth is, I don't remember a lot of that period of my life.

The even sadder truth is that my consumption of booze and pills was on the light end of the scale compared to some guys who had been around longer than me. They were really trapped, and they knew they would never get out. So they escaped another way. When I started to make an assessment of my life back then, I realized that if I stayed long enough, I'd end up just like them. Nowhere to go, and not even remembering where I had been.

It's not the pro wrestling business itself that's the real problem, it's the lifestyle that goes along with it.

The schedule is too demanding for anyone. You have to live on the road, and at the same time deal with the injuries, fans, rental car people, hotel clerks, restaurant waiters and waitresses, company politics, everyone walking around like a zombie, and never being home. And on those rare occasions when you get to go home, you are supposed to suddenly turn it all off and just try to be "Daddy."

Yeah, salesman travel and they are gone a lot, too. But they don't get body-slammed by 250-pound men, or tear up their knees by landing a backflip off the top rope, or have their ribs crushed, or get concussed, or have their arms twisted out of the sockets each night before they head to the airport. Pro wrestlers do, and they are expected to heal on the plane, get a few hours of sleep in a hotel, then show up "looking good" the next night, in the next city.

I found myself getting caught up in everything, and I think I lost sight of reality for a while. But I have no regrets. I chose to jump off the train, move as close to my daughter as possible. Nothing was more important to me than making sure my family life would be stable.

MY FIRST WRESTLEMANIA

KURT ANGLE WAS hurt going into *WrestleMania 2003* in Seattle. He wrenched his neck and it was determined he needed surgery. Kurt didn't want to take a year off, so he found a surgeon in Pittsburgh who had an alternative that involved shaving down the disc instead of the neck-fusion surgery the other wrestlers were getting.

Kurt also didn't want time off for the standard surgery because he wanted to collect that *WrestleMania* main-event payday. I can't say I blame him for that. I wanted that payday, too.

Kurt and I talked a little about our match, but we didn't talk about it much. We knew we could bring out the best in each other, and I knew I had to protect Kurt because his neck was hurt.

John Laurinaitis was going to be the agent for the match. That means he was the choreographer, the guy who had to know what we were going to do, so the cameras could follow us and cover the match properly. The agent carries the finish of the match from Vince, and then talks with the wrestlers, and gets the entire story of the match together. Then he goes back to Vince and hopes Vince likes it.

John wanted to do something special because a lot of corporate eyes were on him since he was being groomed to take over Jim Ross's job as the head of talent relations. He was now the agent for the biggest match of the year, the main event of *WrestleMania*. The WWE title was on the line between two amateur champions, two real wrestlers with legitimate athletic backgrounds. Apparently, that wasn't enough for John Laurinaitis. He thought the match needed a *WrestleMania* moment.

At lunch that day, John came up to me and pitched his great finish, which would see me hit the Shooting Star Press to beat Kurt for the WWE title. John had this elaborate concept of me kicking out of everything Kurt could hit me with. Then Kurt kicks out of the F-5. Since we couldn't beat each other with our best shots, we'd have to dig something out of our bags of tricks. I'd look around, trying to figure out how I could beat Kurt. Then I'd climb to the top rope, and hit the Shooting Star Press to pin Kurt Angle and become a two-time WWE Heavyweight Champion. That was John's big finish, for the biggest match, on the biggest show of the year.

The only problem was that I hadn't done the move for over a year, and it was very dangerous for both of us. A lot can go wrong when a three-hundred-pound man inward-reverse-somersaults himself through the air from the top rope, and the margin for error is slim.

John, however, was relentless, "Brock, you gotta finish the match like that. It's so memorable. It's your *WrestleMania* moment."

I kept thinking my *WrestleMania* moment was beating Kurt, just like I had beaten everyone else, and winning back the title that had been stolen from me at *Survivor Series*. Wasn't that the story we were telling? I didn't want to do the Shooting Star. It didn't make any sense to me.

To crank up the pressure on me a little more, Jim Ross sat down with us, and John started saying, "Don't you think Brock should finish the match with the Shooting Star Press? It's so impressive, no one has seen him do it for such a long time, it's such a great move, blah blah blah."

J.R. thinks about that for a moment and drawls, "Hell, kid, that would be one helluva *WrestleMania* moment!" They had their routine down pat.

Finally, stupidly, I agreed to do it, but I at least wanted to practice the move a few times first. I should have listened to my gut and just said "NO!" But I went down to the ring to practice hurling myself from the top rope.

John got ahold of some crash mats and piled them in the ring for me so I wouldn't hurt myself during practice. When I went off that top rope and threw myself into a reverse spin, it was actually kind of cool. I nailed the landing perfectly my first time. I tried it again, and I nailed it the second time, too. After a few more times, I was really feeling pretty good about it, and we were all thinking it would be no problem when I had to do it at the end of the match.

What I didn't consider was that I was going to be working with Kurt for fifteen to eighteen minutes, and I was probably going to be dead tired and pouring sweat by the time we got around to the finish of the match.

That night, Kurt and I put on the best show possible considering the circumstances. We had a really physical match, which wasn't easy when you think about how injured he was. It finally came time to hit the Shooting Star Press, but Kurt and I had been throwing each other off the ropes and working the corners all night long. When I grabbed the top rope to boost myself up, it was all wet. Not good. As I climbed up, I was dripping even more sweat onto the ropes, but I wasn't thinking about that. Everyone at Safeco Field in Seattle knew what was coming, and they were all screaming for me to hit the move, and beat Kurt Angle for the championship.

There I stood, on the top rope, both arms raised in triumph, my head back, letting the crowd take it all in . . . and then I launched the Shooting Star Press.

Every wrestling fan knows what happened next. My boot slipped off the wet rope, I under-rotated, crashed in spectacular fashion, and gave myself a massive concussion. I damn near broke my neck. I still had enough sense left to know that I had to win, but I don't remember finishing the match. I did finish, which meant I was the champion again, but I sure don't remember it. Not at all.

Can you imagine if I had knocked myself out . . . if that "missed move" had become the finish?

The next morning, I was supposed to do a sponsor appearance, but I couldn't get out of my hotel bed. After I received a few phone calls to rouse me, I finally crawled out and made it down to the appearance. When the sponsor's people saw me throwing up from the aftereffects of the concussion, they sent me back to the hotel.

After you play in the Super Bowl or the World Series, you get some time to yourself, or to take your family on a vacation. Not in pro wrestling. You're right back to work the very next day, doing live TV for *Raw* the first night, or taping *SmackDown!* two nights after *WrestleMania*. Kurt made it through the match, and I was lucky to "only" have suffered a concussion. Kurt went in for the alternative surgery, and I was right back on the road as WWE Champion for the second time.

STARTING YEAR TWO

MY FIRST YEAR on the main roster in WWE was a blur. My second year was even worse. I was running into the grind. Same routine every day, day in and day out. The money was great, and I was buying a lot of nice things, but I had no time to enjoy any of it. That touring schedule just eats you up. I just kept thinking that there has to be a better way to make some real money.

The one good thing—okay, great thing—that came out of my second year was that I got to meet my future wife, Rena.

I think it's pretty common knowledge that I'm a very private man, and there's a reason for that. When I'm on the job, in the ring, at the arena, I'm there to entertain you. I understand that. You paid to see me, and I owe it to you to make sure your money was well spent.

But when I'm not on the job, I don't think I owe anything to anybody. If you're a plumber, and you're out to dinner with your family, would you like it if the waiter walked up and said, "Hey, the toilet just backed up, can you come in the back and fix it?" Probably not. You are there to eat, not to fish tampons out of the drain pipe.

When I'm enjoying some time with my family, I'm not at work. I'm not "on." I'm not there to entertain anyone. I'm a husband and a father. I'm Daddy. That's who I am, and all I want to be. So if some jackass wants to pose for pictures with me, it really burns my ass because he isn't just imposing on me, he is imposing on my wife and my children, too.

I think everyone should have a right to privacy. Certainly, my family has a right to be left alone. My wife was on TV for a while, so she can expect some of the attention, I get that. But my children aren't performers. What makes them fair game? What gives anyone else the right to take pictures of my children? Why does anyone think it's okay to just walk up to me and act as if I owe them an answer to personal questions? Is it because they bought a ticket or purchased a pay-per-view? I've never been able to grasp that. Why can't I just do my job? If I'm at an event, or out promoting something, that's one thing. I expect to take pictures and sign autographs. That's why I'm there. But I deserve a private life, too, and so does my family.

Over the years, I'm sure that being as private as I am has cost me a lot of money. I could be like one of those media whores that shows up anywhere there might be a camera just to keep my name out there, and to keep my face on the TV and in the papers so the endorsements will keep coming in. But that's not me, and I can live with that.

I like to stay home, spend time with my family, and be left alone. My life is my life. It's nobody's business what goes on in my house, or with my wife or my children. I won't intrude on your private life. Don't intrude on mine.

That's why, in some ways, the WWE character I envied the most was Kane. He had the greatest gig ever, because he was a big star who wore a mask on TV. When he went home, he'd get to take off the mask and live a normal life. Nobody knew what he looked like, and no one ever bothered him when he went about his personal life. He must have had about as normal a life as you can have in professional wrestling. That's probably why Glenn Jacobs (Kane) survived for so long in WWE. Maybe I should have worn a mask. I might have lasted just a little longer . . . or not.

THE GRIND

WHEN PEOPLE TALK to me about 2003, they talk about my match with Kurt at *WrestleMania*; my matches with John Cena and Big Show; the Iron Man Match (most falls in sixty minutes) I had with Kurt on *SmackDown!*; or me beating Kurt for the title and turning heel again.

Financially, that was also my best year in WWE. I was made champion so fast, Vince never even got around to giving me a new contract. I was on the road so much, we never had the time to discuss a new deal. Even by the time I was already a two-time champion, I was still working under the "developmental contract" I signed when I was recruited to train in OVW. Finally, we got around to discussing a new contract, and I signed a major deal with WWE on July 1, 2003.

Jim Ross kept telling me I had joined the millionaire's club faster than anyone else in the history of the business. That may be true, but I'll have to take his word for it because I didn't pay much attention to what the other guys were making. They all lied anyway, so who really knew?

I was making a shitload of money, but I just couldn't imagine being on the road for another fifteen years or so. I really liked the boys, but I didn't want to be like them. It didn't take me long to figure that out.

It's so hard to even imagine being thirty-five to forty years old, working matches four nights a week in four different cities. When those wrestlers get home for a day or two, they are too tired and banged up to do anything. The few who still have families try to give their loved ones a little quality time, but when they arrive at home tired, hurt, and probably hungover, they end up spending the first day just decompressing. Then they use the next day to catch up on the mail, the bills, and chores around the house. Once they've had a night or two in their own beds, they are packed and off to the airport piss-early the next morning. Their wives and kids get to see them on TV. So what? That's no substitute for being there.

It makes no difference where the plane lands, because all the cities look the same. It bears repeating. All the hotel rooms look the same. All the locker rooms, rental car return lots, shuttle buses, they all look the same. You're on autopilot all the time. Then you go home, but before you know it, you're back in the grind, shaking everyone's hands, being careful not to piss anyone off.

Vince drills into the guys the notion that they have to believe in their characters if they want the fans to believe in them, too. What happens over the years is that some of the guys get so into their characters, they don't know when—or how—to turn it off. They become their own number one fans. That's how Vince gets so many guys by the balls after a while. The guys will do anything to get their characters over, and if they're lucky enough to get into a good position, they will do anything to keep their characters in the spotlight. It becomes all about Vince. Vince pulls and controls all of the strings.

Vince can suggest anything he wants, and as long as he says, "It will be great for your character," there's a bunch of guys ready and willing to do whatever he says. They are brainwashed, and they don't even know it.

Take a shot to the head with a metal folding chair? Great idea. Do a body slam from the top rope onto the concrete outside the ring? Awesome finish. Fall from the top of a twelve-foot ladder? That'll get a big pop. Finish the match with a Shooting Star Press? Yeah, I know.

Even though I was there only a relatively short time, I wasn't immune to the sell. I was slowly getting sucked in. WWE superstar Brock Lesnar agreed to do the Shooting Star Press finish, not Brock Lesnar, farmer and father.

The problem is that when you are in WWE's universe, it becomes very difficult to step out. You can't see in from the outside. You can't take an honest look at yourself and say, "What the hell am I doing?" There is no such thing as "normal."

In an attempt to keep my sanity, and avoid becoming like all the others, I kept telling J.R., Laurinaitis, Brisco (and anyone else who would listen) that I needed some time off. That didn't work, so I finally cornered Vince and told him the same thing.

You should have seen the look on his face. You would have thought that I stuck a knife in his stomach and twisted it. He acted as if I had committed the ultimate act of betrayal. "I have all of this TV time invested in you" . . . "The COMPANY is counting on you" . . . "I told everyone I could rely on you. You can't let me down."

Eventually, I persuaded Vince to give me a weekend off here and there, but he was never going to let me come off the road for a couple of months. It didn't matter to him if I dropped the title or not, there was just no way he was going to give me that kind of time off.

Vince did, of course, have a lot riding on me. I was the youngest champion ever, and was built up to be the Next Big Thing. But a lot of it was also Vince making sure I didn't step outside of the WWE universe long enough to be able to look back in. If I did, I might see things as they are, and not as he wanted me to see them.

It's all about control, and Vince wasn't going to let me have any. The more I work, the more money I generate for Vince through ticket sales, merchandise, DVDs, pay-per-views, and advertising revenue. If it ruins my life, and I end up a zombie like the others, so what.

On one of the rare weekends that I did manage to get off, I was sitting at home, and I was trying to figure out why I was so worn down. I felt like an old man even though I was only twenty-five. The obvious suspects were the injuries that had never had time to heal properly; a lot of empty vodka bottles; the hundreds of pain pills I was swallowing just to get through the tour; and the fact that I was never home and was losing my family connections because of it. I was a professional wrestler all right.

But still I thought maybe if I didn't have to deal with some of the travel hassles it might be different. Lines at airport security were getting worse and worse after 9/11, and for a lot of flights you had to arrive two hours early. When you fly every day, and you are always tired and beat-up, the constant lines and waiting around just wears on you. And it is even worse when you can't walk through an airport without being recognized by hundreds or thousands of people who want pictures and autographs. So I ran the numbers, and I found out it was costing Vince about $175,000 a year to fly me all over the country. The international tours were a different story, but just the domestic travel was somewhere between $150,000 and $175,000.

Then it hit me. What if I bought my own plane, and avoided all the lines, check-ins, time spent waiting to board, walking through the airport, getting my bags? What if I could just hop on my own plane, go to work, do my job, and get back on my plane and come home? It would be just like driving to work for most people. Yeah, I could do that!

So I added up some more numbers, and I figured it out so that I could buy my own plane, have one of my oldest friends, Justin, fly it for me, and actually save Vince money at the same time. Vince would only need to pay for maintenance and fuel, and he would come out ahead. One day during a *SmackDown!* taping, I went into Vince's office with my spreadsheets and told him my plan. I showed Vince how he'd actually save money making this deal with me, and maybe I wouldn't need as much time off as I was looking for. Wouldn't you know it, the very next day the son of a bitch got back to me and said, "Let's do it!"

By September 2003, I had dropped the title back to Kurt Angle, only to "turn heel" in order to "beat" him for the title again. I wasn't even a full year and a half into my run, and I was WWE Champion for the third time. I wasn't a mark for the title, but I was very happy to grab the championship so I could be in more main events. I was already making millions. I had my own plane. The company was counting on me, and I was being reminded of that every day.

Then came Miami . . .

BROCK VS. ROCK IN MIAMI

I **WAS SO** excited the day I heard that I had been booked against Dwayne "The Rock" Johnson in Miami for our second one-on-one match (and if we're including the Triple Threat Match with HHH in Australia, our third match overall). It ended up being one of the most important days in my pro wrestling career, because that match in Miami was a pivotal point in my decision to quit WWE.

Before that first *SummerSlam*, the company flew me down to Miami so Dwayne and I could work out the high points and the finish of our upcoming match. It was Dwayne's daughter's first birthday, and he invited me to stay in his home, with him and his family.

Dwayne's dad was a journeyman wrestler named Rocky Johnson, so he knew how to play the pro wrestling game as good as anyone. Just like Curt Hennig, Dwayne was born into the business. These second-generation wrestlers, and even third-generation wrestlers like Randy Orton understand the business a lot better than guys who break in from other walks of life, because they grew up around it. Dwayne, Curt, and Randy all saw what the business was about, and the sacrifices a family has to make. They also learned the psychology behind the scenes because they were exposed to it from day one. That's a tremendous advantage for them, because it might as well be in their blood.

I wasn't born into the business, so unlike Dwayne and the others, I had to learn the hard way about a lot of things.

If someone from the company would have called me and said, "Hey Brock, would you mind doing a job for the Rock this weekend in Miami?" it wouldn't have been a big deal to me. I owed him that much. I liked Dwayne, and I learned a lot from him that week before he put me over for the championship. But the way everything was handled in Miami really opened my eyes to the wrestling business, and the night of my big match with Dwayne is one that I will never forget.

I showed up at the arena and was met by Jack Lanza, the road agent in charge of the show. Jack was a Minnesota boy and took me under his wing when I moved up to the WWE main roster. As the road agent, Jack would get the finishes on the phone or via e-mail from Vince, or J.R., or Laurinaitis. He would then produce the live event, and report back to the bosses on how the show went, who performed well, and who didn't.

I had been up and down the road with Jack a few times, so this day shouldn't have been any different from any other. I figured when the time was right, we would all sit down, and Jack would tell us how Vince wanted the match to end. No reason to believe this show was any different from all the others, except I was working with Dwayne, and that was pretty special for the both of us.

Then I realized: "Something ain't right here."

The show had already started, and Jack hadn't given us a finish yet. Dwayne and I started talking about our match, and I kept thinking "Okay, but what's the finish here?"

It was about an hour and a half before we were supposed to step into the ring for the main event of the evening, and Dwayne says to me, ". . . and that's when I'll hit you with the Rock Bottom, one . . . two . . . three!"

I actually laughed, because I thought Dwayne was ribbing me. I was the WWE Champion. The Golden Boy. It was my time to be on top. I was supposed to win. And here's the Rock, who should know better, saying he's going to pin the WWE Champion with the Rock Bottom. That was funny.

Dwayne had this nervous look on his face, and he wasn't laughing with me. He just put all the heat on Vince right away, and said, "I can't believe Vince didn't tell you . . . didn't he call you about this?" Dwayne made it seem like he thought I knew he was supposed to beat me, and that he was shocked I didn't.

"I told you about things like this," Dwayne said. "A lot of shit falls through the cracks, you gotta stay on top of Vince about everything."

I remember the week I stayed with Dwayne, he was on the phone with Vince constantly. It was the right way to handle his business. Dwayne had a hand in everything they did with his character. He was a big enough star that he had some say in how his character was used, and how Vince would market and promote him. Even back then, Dwayne would tell me, "Now that you're going to be on top, you need to stay on top of everything, all the time."

So I went to Lanza and said, "Jack, tell me what the hell is going on here . . . I'm the WWE Champion, and I'm losing tonight? Why didn't anyone tell me?" Jack's only reply was, "Well, it's a non-title match!"

What the hell did that mean? I never knew that my title wasn't on the line that night. I never knew that I was supposed to lose to the Rock.

"It's Miami," Jack said. "No one will ever know!"

I can remember hearing Jack say that like it was yesterday. I wasn't upset about losing. That wasn't the point at all. What bothered me was that I was the last guy to know, when I should have been the first. No one had the guts to tell me the truth, until it was time to step into the ring. Just from the look on Dwayne's face and the tone in Jack's voice, I knew they were in on something I wasn't. It was obvious to me that Vince, Dwayne and Jack were all in cahoots, and I wasn't being smartened up to the situation until the very last minute.

That night changed my attitude toward the WWE, because it's when I started to feel Vince was a manipulating bastard, and that I was being played.

I thought it was a stupid decision to have the WWE Champion lose in a "non-title match," but that was something I was going to have to accept. As someone who fights for real, it made no sense to me for the champion to lose ... and still be the champion. If someone can beat the champ, then they deserve the title. It's that simple.

Who wants to see that? People pay to see the champion because he's the champion, and his position as number one is on the line. I didn't like it. I had been pulling the company plow, been filling the arenas and selling the pay-per-views, and no one even tells me that Dwayne wants to get his loss back? No one has the balls to just say, "Brock, this is the way it is"?

Vince can't tell me the angle, the story, and why it makes sense for me to lay down for the Rock in a "non-title" match? He doesn't want my two cents' worth? I'm the damn poster boy for this company, and I'm the only one who doesn't know what's going on?

Even though I knew one day I would have to do a job for The Rock, I still kept thinking that Vince was really screwing with me, and that there was a lot more behind keeping me in the dark than just Dwayne wanting to get his loss back after a year and a half. Did

I do something to piss Vince off? Did he need to show that he could keep me in my place? Something was going on.

I'll be the first one to admit that I'm a control freak. When it comes to business, I want to know what's going on, when, where, and why. This is my living. If I have to lose for the good of the company, I will, but it'll be on my terms. I thought I had a good relationship with Vince, but obviously I was wrong.

When it came to my business with the WWE, the one person I thought I could trust was Vince. When I first started we had that handshake, and I put my future in his hands. He ran the company. He controlled everything. I knew that if I couldn't count on him to tell it to me straight, I was screwed. I could play the game with everybody else on the roster and in the office, but I couldn't play games with the owner of the company. That's a fight I'm going to lose every time because HE writes the checks. HE makes all the rules.

If I'm Vince's top guy . . . the guy he's relying on . . . his go-to guy . . . his main event . . . why would he lie to me? Why would he play this kind of game with me, in Miami, for no reason? Just to mess with my head? Just to do it for the sake of doing it?

To Vince, it may have been just another day in the wrestling business, but to me it was a lot more than that. That day was the first in a chain of events that led to my departure from the WWE.

The wheels were still spinning in my head about getting screwed over in Miami, when Vince tells me he wants me to lose the WWE title to Eddie Guerrero. Of course, Vince put his own twist on it: "Goldberg's going to interfere, give the win to Eddie, and that'll set up this huge match at *WrestleMania* between the two of you. Lesnar vs. Goldberg is so big it will sell itself, you don't need the WWE title involved."

Of course, Vince kept telling me how good it would be for my character to drop the title to Eddie, and then take on Goldberg. "You can beat Goldberg in thirty seconds. He's leaving, so I don't care. We can get Austin involved, and it's going to be the biggest match on the card. *WrestleMania 20*. Madison Square Garden. Brock Lesnar vs. Bill Goldberg, and Stone Cold Steve Austin will be out there as the special guest referee. It's big box office, it's pure money."

I knew what this was about. Vince was selling me hard on *WrestleMania* because he wanted to get the title on Eddie Guerrero. Vince kept telling me how the Latino audience was growing, and this was the right move for business. But after what happened in Miami, our relationship had already gone south. I never believed another word that came out of Vince's mouth. I no longer had any faith whatsoever in the Federation.

But Vince isn't the only one that screwed me.

LEAVING WWE

I WAS GETTING angrier and angrier. I couldn't get any time off. My body was hurting. I was going through a lot of personal drama. I was pissed off about the way things went down in Miami, and I certainly wasn't happy about being replaced by Eddie Guerrero as WWE Champion.

I remembered how every step up the ladder was worth more money to me, and now I'm looking at going back down that ladder?

I don't talk to a lot of people from the company nowadays, and it was the same story during my time in WWE. I didn't like how untrustworthy so many of the boys were, but I thought there were a few people I could count on. Kurt Angle was supposed to be one of those people. Then something happened that caused me to wonder.

I had many conversations with Kurt, but I soon found out those conversations didn't remain strictly between us. It's unfortunate I had to learn that lesson the hard way.

I knew that at any given moment, anybody in that locker room would stab you in the back if they could get away with it. They all wanted a better place on the card. Everyone wanted to make more money, to have the best matches, get the biggest push. It's no secret in the pro wrestling business that you have to watch your back at all times. Everyone is put in the position to double-cross the other guy to get ahead. Sometimes, they want to see if you're willing to be that ruthless, because Vince likes to see his top guys fight for the number one position.

Kurt and I should have had a bond. We both rose to the top in amateur wrestling. We were both real athletes, true competitors. But at the same time, Kurt wanted my position just like everyone else in the locker room. He just wanted what I had.

Vince never looked at Kurt the way he looked at me. Kurt had that Olympic Gold Medal, but Vince and HHH didn't see an Olympic Champion. They only saw a five-foot nine-inch guy in tights. In their minds, fans pay to see the huge guys perform. Kurt could never be "bigger than life." It didn't matter how good he was in the ring, Kurt just wasn't tall enough or big enough to be Vince McMahon's top guy for any length of time.

Believing I could trust Kurt, I told him I was thinking of getting out of the business. I didn't tell anyone else, and he said he wouldn't either. But soon after I confided in him, I became convinced that Vince knew I was planning to leave. Did Kurt stooge me out?

At the time, Kurt and I were traveling together, and I was already thinking something was up with him just from the way he was acting. Then, one day, I went out to move the rental car, and saw Kurt's cell phone on the seat next to me. I opened it up, and the last call made was to Vince McMahon. Does that prove anything? Maybe, maybe not. But from that day forward I kept my mouth shut, and didn't say anything to Kurt that I didn't want anyone else to know.

I dropped the WWE title to Eddie Guerrero at the Cow Palace in San Francisco. The whole story line was centered on Bill Goldberg getting into the ring and giving me a spear. I didn't believe Vince wanted the title on Eddie Guerrero because he thought Eddie would draw more money than I could, or that Vince had this vision in his head about me versus Goldberg at *WrestleMania*. I suspected Vince made the decision to take the title off me because Kurt had told him I was thinking about leaving.

I started to concentrate on just getting through *WrestleMania*, and getting my hands on that nice payday before getting out. You know it never works out that way, of course, because just as I was getting my head into survival mode, WWE pulled another bullshit move on me.

We were scheduled to go to South Africa, and that's just a miserable trip. It's on the other side of the world. The food sucks. It's a long trip to get there, and a long trip back. There's nothing good about it except you can make some good money when you're in the main event.

I was scheduled to wrestle in those main events against Kurt and Eddie in Triple Threat matches for all four South Africa shows, but right before we left the United States, the WWE changed the main events to just Kurt vs. Eddie. I was told the two of them needed to get their match down for *WrestleMania*, which meant I was stuck wrestling Bob Holly, who I had just beat in four minutes at *The Royal Rumble*.

I like Bob. He's a good guy and he takes his shit seriously, but I didn't want to work with him. Nothing against him, but wrestling Bob Holly wasn't worth anything to me at the time.

We did our match at *The Royal Rumble*, and that should have been the end of our story line. But now I have to travel all the way to South Africa to work with Bob Holly? Could anyone please tell me why? I knew no one would pay to see that match. Since I'm not really needed, give me some time off. I really needed the break by this time, but John Laurinaitis told me how much I'm needed on the card. AGAINST BOB HOLLY? Are you shitting me?

I knew the truth. I was just on the card, taking up space. That's not where I wanted to be. It's never where I wanted to be.

Even today, at this very moment, I'm still pissed at myself for getting on the plane to South Africa. I should have just walked. The trip sucked all around, the money wasn't worth the time and aggravation, and I drank all the way back to the United States. I spent fifty-four miserable hours on an airplane that trip.

When we landed at JFK Airport in New York, we got herded like cattle onto a bus over to LaGuardia Airport, where we were supposed to get on another plane and head to Atlanta. Once we get to Atlanta, we're supposed to take this little puddle jumper to Savannah. Once the crew would get to Savannah, it's back to the same old monotonous daily grind again. Get your bags. Grab a rental car. Find a gym. Look for something to eat. Hope for some sleep, because you have to be ready the next morning to spend your whole day taping TV.

That's when I snapped.

Nathan Jones had lost his mind a month earlier, and he was just minutes away from wrestling in his hometown in Australia. But the weird thing is that, when Nathan snapped, I kept thinking that everything he was saying made sense.

"Nothing is worth this stress" . . . "It's all games, but then they tell you how seriously they take their own business" . . . "I just don't want to be here anymore."

So we land at JFK and get bussed over to LaGuardia, and that's when I started drinking again. I was sitting at the airport bar, and I decided right then and there that I wasn't going to get on yet another airplane and go all the way to Savannah. Why? So I could wrestle Bob Holly again? I had no idea what they had in store for me at the

TV taping, and I didn't care. I had enough. This was it. The end of the line. I was going home.

I got up from the bar, walked through the airport to the ticket desk, and bought my own plane ticket to Minneapolis. When I got on the plane headed home, I ordered another drink to celebrate, but they cut me off. I wasn't happy about being refused alcohol, and I almost caused a major scene that could have turned out really ugly. Not a smart move on my part, but when your head is all full with this other nonsense . . .

Lucky for me I wasn't kicked off the plane and I made it home. Those poor flight attendants. They could have blown the whistle on me, but they didn't. I guess this is my chance to say "I'm sorry" in a pretty public way to them, and thanks for not making a bad day a whole lot worse.

I had it in my head that I wasn't going to do the TV taping in Savannah. In fact, I was going to pull a Steve Austin. I was home, and I wasn't leaving again. Not to go back on the road. No way that was going to happen! This is where I can say I really understood what Austin was thinking that day he walked out, and why I never took it personally. When Steve walked out, it wasn't about working with me. It was about everything *but* me.

I didn't want to leave because of Eddie Guerrero, or Bob Holly, or anyone else. I just had to get out. I had lost my faith, which happened because I had no family after being on the road three hundred days a year, and all I had was the Federation. How could I provide a nice life for my daughter if she never got a chance to see me? And what kind of financial rewards could I earn if I am slowly being worked back down the ladder? I was finally thinking clearly, or so I thought.

I don't know why I got on my plane the next morning and flew to Savannah, but I did. I think Rena talked me into it. "Go to Savannah, settle up face-to-face with Vince, handle your business the right way."

I love that woman.

When I showed up at the building in Savannah, the producer told me I was supposed to go nine minutes on TV with Bob Holly. I blew a gasket. I went straight to Gerry Brisco, and told him, "You recruited me, so I want you to know I'm leaving. I'm outta here."

I wanted to tell Vince to his face, too. I had dropped the title to Eddie Guerrero so WWE could draw with the Latino market, and my match with Goldberg at *WrestleMania* is supposed to be so big the title isn't needed to sell it? I'm supposed to crush Bill Goldberg at *Mania* in thirty seconds, but I can't get through Bob Holly in nine minutes?

I remember watching Brisco look for Vince, and I was just boiling. Vince was in the ring with HHH, so I just walked up to him and said, "We need to chat." Not understanding how serious I was, Vince made me wait a few minutes. I was only getting hotter and hotter, so I interrupted his conversation and told him we needed to sit down and talk immediately.

We went into his office, and I told Vince I was done, "going home." I had no desire to wrestle Bob Holly on TV, didn't want to wrestle that night period, and just wanted to leave. Vince said, "Well, Brock, what about *WrestleMania*? You can't leave on bad terms that way!"

I'll never forget his next line. "You can't do this to me."

All I could think of was, "DO THIS TO YOU?" I didn't know what Vince thought I was doing to him, but whatever was going on was something I no longer wanted any part of!

I agreed to stay on through *WrestleMania*, but only because I wanted that payday from my match with Goldberg. I trimmed down my match on TV with Bob Holly to a few minutes, wrestled that night, got showered and dressed, and jumped back on my plane.

Rena rode home on my plane with me, and I felt relieved. I was going to leave the company. Stupid me, I let Vince talk me into dragging it out all the way to *WrestleMania*, but if I didn't agree to that, they probably wouldn't have paid me a lot of the money they owed me already. So financially, it was smart to agree to stay through *Mania*.

I know Vince was pissed off. In his universe, I was ungrateful. I had turned around and spit in his face. But it's not like he shouldn't have seen it coming. How many times did I tell him I needed time off? How many times did I tell him I wasn't happy with the life, or what it was doing to me? Vince always had his stock reply: "Brock, you're so much tougher than that."

But it wasn't about being tough. It was about having a life. A year or two bouncing around town to town, bar to bar, girl to girl, Vicodin to Vicodin, vodka bottle to vodka bottle, is not a life.

I loved being in the ring and performing. Bringing people to their feet. Getting people to hate my character. Entertaining the fans. I had a great time doing all of that, especially when I got to work with people I liked. But I wanted to have a family, too, and I knew there was no way to do that with the schedule I worked. I don't hate professional wrestling, and I certainly don't hate the people in it. Life on the road is just not for me. It's not the life I choose to live.

When the time came, I made my announcement and told everyone I was leaving the WWE. From that day forward I became the outcast. None of the guys wanted to be seen with me, because I was the bad apple. I was turning my back on the wrestling business—their business, their life. I was leaving. I was jumping off the train. They couldn't understand it, because that train was the only ride most of these guys would ever know.

I didn't care, because I had made my choice. I still walked around like I owned the place, because there wasn't one guy in that company who could even hold my jockstrap. If I wanted to shoot on anyone in that locker room at any time, there wasn't a thing anyone could have done about it. I could have stretched every single one of them out. But that's not what the business is about, so I tried to be good about it. Be a professional. Do my job. Earn my check. Be a provider for my family.

My daughter, Mya, changed my life. I wanted to be there for her, wanted to watch her grow up. So many of these guys, with their multiple ex-wives, and broken-up families in different states, missed everything that's really important in life. I didn't want that, and I didn't want that for my daughter either. She deserves a real father.

Don't get me wrong. There were a lot of good things about working for WWE. I made a lot of money, even though I spent quite a bit of it trying to get out of my contract. I became famous, which did help me when I wanted a chance in the UFC. I learned about promotion and marketing. But the best thing was meeting my wife. If I hadn't been in WWE, I wouldn't have met Rena. She's given me two healthy sons, and she's been wonderful with Mya. When I say I'm a man who has been blessed by God, I mean it.

Rena stood by my decision to leave WWE, which wasn't easy for her because she was still with the company at the time. But she could tell there was no way I was going to stay any longer. Besides the lifestyle and all the bullshit, I wanted to compete and get back into athletics again. I thought maybe I would give pro football a try.

But, in my desperation to get out of WWE, I made the biggest mistake of my life. I signed a release that included a noncompete clause.

Vince was pissed at me because we had just done the new deal in July 2003, and he claimed it was the best deal he ever gave any wrestler. But by then I didn't care about the money or the contract. I had money, and I just wanted to be done with Vince.

At the time, I didn't know I was going to pursue a career in mixed martial arts, or try to get into UFC. I had no idea I was going to wrestle in Japan. I thought I was headed into the NFL, but that wasn't the main thing on my mind. All I could think about was getting away from Vince, and escaping the WWE lifestyle. Everything else was secondary.

Vince finally said he would let me go, but he wanted me to sign a release agreement. This time, I thought it would probably be a good idea to have my lawyer look at the document before I signed it. I was sitting in a hotel somewhere when I got the release from Vince, and I faxed it to my lawyer in Minneapolis. He called me, said he would look at it, and then would fax back a marked-up copy to discuss with me.

But I got impatient. I just wanted out. I never intended to compete with Vince and WWE, and I didn't care if Vince's agreement said I couldn't. So before my attorney even had a chance to comment, I signed Vince's release. I thought it would be quick and easy, I would get my *WrestleMania* payday, and I'd be done with pro wrestling forever. I couldn't have been more wrong.

What I didn't know, because I didn't wait to hear back from my lawyer, is that while my WWE contract had a one-year noncompete clause, the release I signed was much different.

Just to avoid the hassles of lawyers negotiating and everything that happens when you're leaving, I signed a release that stated I couldn't appear for any wrestling, ultimate fighting, or "sports entertainment" companies, anywhere in the world, until mid-2010.

With one stroke of the pen, I royally screwed myself over. I went from not being able to wrestle in TNA (Vince's only televised U.S. competitor) for a year, to not being able to wrestle, fight, or do anything in "sports entertainment" worldwide for almost six years. I had just turned twenty-seven years old. If I didn't fight that non-compete clause, I would have been forced to stay out of work until I was thirty-three . . . which happens to be my age at the time I'm writing this book. Everything I've accomplished since that final match at Madison Square Garden with Bill Goldberg would never have happened. The prime of my career would have been spent sitting on the bench.

I guess the old expression "you live and you learn" applies here. It cost me nearly a year and a lot of money to fight that noncompete clause. But that's in the past, and I won my freedom. I have my family. I love my life. I don't walk around thinking about it. It's the past. That part of my life is over.

CLOSURE

IT'S FITTING THAT my last match in WWE was against Bill Goldberg, and the referee was Steve Austin, because Bill and Steve are two guys I really like. It's a shame that I didn't get to know either one of them very well until after we all got out of the business.

Steve's a good guy. I thought Steve was going to be a WWE Lifer, but he surprised me and everyone else. I don't have any regrets about my time in WWE, and I certainly don't have any regrets about leaving, but I sometimes wish that Steve and I had one match during the time our paths crossed. That would have been interesting, because his character and my character would have been natural enemies. That makes for great box office.

Steve had this rough edge to him, a no-bullshit kind of guy. He was also a lot more into the politics than I was. I was always so black and white on every issue, but Steve could always find some gray. Steve and I could have drawn a lot of money against each other. That would have been something special. Who knows? Maybe one day, we'll do it.

I had no problem laying down for Bill Goldberg for my final match, even though I had been told I was set up to squash him in thirty seconds. I guess they were more pissed at me for leaving than they were pissed at Bill for doing the same thing.

Bill wasn't Vince's guy. To Vince, Bill was a WCW creation, a carpetbagger. So Bill got to spear me and beat me at *WrestleMania*. But no one in the Garden cared. They were too busy booing us both out of the building because they knew we were leaving. The best part of the match was Austin stunning us.

Bill's my kind of guy. Neither of us wanted to be in the ring that last night—we just wanted to collect our checks and be done. It wouldn't have mattered if we had been buddies and had hung out together in WWE, because you're so numb there anyway, you have to take everything with a grain of salt. It's better that we got to know each other away from there, because that's when we both realized we could have a friendship. In WWE, we were just two big miserable SOBs. Once we were both outside of the company, we realized we had a lot in common.

Bill is a straight-up guy who got in to get out. I respect that. He wants to do a job he enjoys. You know that Bill could be sitting in the TNA locker room right now, milking every paycheck he can get out of them just like the other so-called "legends." But that's not Bill. He wanted to play with his son, work on his cars, and do a few TV spots for cash. Bill was the ringside commentator for my first MMA fight, and we've been good friends ever since.

It's funny that we were both "seek and destroy" behemoths in pro wrestling, and wrapped it up together at *WrestleMania*. I never spent any time with Bill before that last day, but because he was so cool, I was open to us becoming friends once we got out.

So, I did *WrestleMania*, and I went home in March 2004—no longer a champion, and no longer a pro wrestler. I was about to try my hand at the NFL.

PART III

THE SWORD AT MY THROAT

MY BRIEF NFL EXPERIENCE

AFTER GETTING OUT of WWE in the spring of 2004, I started chasing after a career in the NFL. But it didn't matter what sport I was going after. I was escaping the WWE lifestyle. The NFL made sense to me. It was legitimate competition, and I wanted to compete.

I went shopping for a football agent, and the first person I called was a guy by the name of Mike Morris, who was a longtime long-snapper for the Minnesota Vikings. Back when I was wrestling for the Gophers, I met Mike through the Fellowship of Christian Athletes. I was invited out to his MILO gym to lift some weights. That gym got a lot of notoriety, because Mike would talk about it all the time on KFAN radio in Minneapolis. In case you're wondering, *MILO* stands for "Mike's Insane Lifting Order."

Mike Morris and I hit it off pretty good because we were both guys who just loved to crank up the music in the gym and do squats until we were bleeding out of our noses. My weight-training routine at the University of Minnesota was my own program, and I started training with Mike in between my junior and senior year. I looked up to Mike because he was successful, had a good family, nice kids, nice wife, a very decent life.

The MILO Gym was in Mike's basement. His whole basement was a gym. Since I knew Mike, he knew he could be honest with me. In that first phone call, he couldn't believe I was getting out of WWE. "You must be nuts!" he said. "You want to walk away from a sure thing, guaranteed millions of dollars for ten years, so you can go after something that has maybe a five percent chance for you to make the transition? You haven't played football since high school!"

I appreciated his honesty.

I told Mike I was serious. I had jumped off the train and I was done with WWE. I wanted to pursue this goal, and I was going to give it my all. Mike accepted everything I told him, and told me he would be 100 percent behind me. He proved that to be a truthful statement because he introduced me to John Wolf, who used to represent a few NBA players and a few NFL players, but was now kind of out of the mix. He referred me to Ed Hitchcock.

Ed was a Minnesota boy, a University of Minnesota grad, and a sports agent. I liked him, so we went to work right away. Ed put this game plan together. "You gotta get in football shape," he told me, "so we need to get you down to Arizona as soon as possible. There's a facility down there called Athlete's Performance, where all of the top NFL players, and top athletes from all over the world, go."

I took Ed's advice and headed south. When I got down there, one of the first guys I met was a midwestern boy named Luke Richesson. He grew up on the Kansas-Missouri border, and was one of the trainers. Luke did a little wrestling and had played some college football,

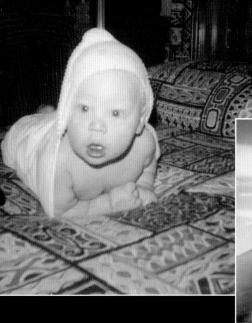

Even as a toddler, I was
always ready to grapple.

This could have been a
different career path . . .

I was always into athletic endeavors.

I was a happy kid!

Even as a kid, I always felt at home being a wrestler.

I owe everything to my mom and dad.

Junior College Champion at Bismarck State in 1998.

Winning for Bismarck State.

285

2000 NCAA
WRESTLING CHAMPIONSHIPS
hosted by
UNIVERSITY OF MISSOURI and
ST. LOUIS SPORTS COMMISSION

Winning the NCAA
Division I Heavyweight
Championship.
*(Courtesy of the
University of Minnesota)*

With Paul in WWE . . .
Here Comes The
Pain! *(Courtesy of
Baseball Magazine-Sha,
Weekly ProWrestling/
Fumi Saito)*

I respected Ric Flair's contributions to the business, but I didn't want to grow up to be like him. *(Courtesy of Baseball Magazine-Sha, Weekly ProWrestling/Fumi Saito)*

I liked working with RVD. He never complained. Neither did I.
(Courtesy of Baseball Magazine-Sha, Weekly ProWrestling/Fumi Saito)

I have to say,
Hulk put me
over in a very
big way.
(Courtesy of
Baseball
Magazine-Sha,
Weekly
ProWrestling/
Fumi Saito)

Moments after beating The Rock for the WWE Undisputed Title.
I'm a much richer man in this picture than I was two minutes before it was taken!
(Courtesy of Baseball Magazine-Sha, Weekly ProWrestling/Fumi Saito)

Vince wanted me to be "King Kong on top of the cage" after defeating the Undertaker in the Hell in a Cell Match. *(Courtesy of Baseball Magazine-Sha, Weekly ProWrestling/Fumi Saito)*

Me as a babyface hitting the F-5 on Paul.
(Courtesy of Baseball Magazine-Sha, Weekly ProWrestling/Fumi Saito)

My *WrestleMania* Moment. This is not going to end well!   *(Courtesy of Gregory Davis)*

Concussed, but WWE Champion once again! *(Courtesy of Baseball Magazine-Sha, Weekly ProWrestling/Fumi Saito)*

This is the moment Steve Mazzagatti called a foul in my first fight with Frankie. *(Scott Peterson/ MMAWeekly.com)*

The punch that ended Heath Her█ ██ ███
(Photograph by Josh Hedges/Zuf

The Octagon is the Ultimate proving ground! (Photograph by Jon Kopaloff/FilmMagic)

Ground and pound on Randy Couture en route to winning the UFC Title. *(Photograph by Josh Hedges/Zuffa LLC via Getty Images)*

With my wife, Rena, after beating Couture for the UFC Title. I owe that woman so much! *(Photograph by Jon Kopaloff/Getty Images*

There's just something so relaxing about punching Frankie in the face.
(Scott Peterson/MMAWeekly.com)

Getting up in Frankie's face after *UFC 100*.   *(Scott Peterson/MMAWeekly.com)*

Celebrating with Marty after overcoming Shane Carwin's onslaught at *UFC 116*.
(Photograph by Josh Hedges/Zuffa LLC/Zuffa LLC via Getty Images)

but he just lacked size. Luke more than made up for that, though, because he was a stick of dynamite.

Today, Luke is the head strength coach for the Jacksonville Jaguars, and he's also my strength and conditioning coach. I consider Luke one of the vital members of Team DeathClutch.

When I got down to Phoenix, I stayed at the Marriott for a little while, but that got old fast. It was like being in the wrestling business that I had just escaped, sleeping in a hotel every night. So I rented a condo and started getting my head into the game.

I got up every day, ate breakfast, and put everything I had into Luke's conditioning program. My whole life was about working out. In the meantime, Rena was still on the road with WWE, and she was flying into Phoenix to be with me. I didn't like the fact that she was in that environment anymore. I already knew she was the woman that I wanted to be with for the rest of my life, but she wasn't ready to let go of her career yet.

I guess I can't really blame Rena for not walking out when I did. We weren't married, I had just made myself unemployed, and the odds of a guy who never played college football making an NFL roster were not good. But none of that stopped me from trying to get her to quit.

I hated it when Rena was on the road. There is a lot of testosterone in the business, and I was worried about what some jackass might do or say to her. But Rena is a remarkable woman, and she can take care of herself. She did finally leave the WWE, but not because they were treating her wrong or anything like that. She didn't do it because they disrespected her. She left for me. My wife is an amazing woman.

Training for a football career I didn't yet have was a little weird for me. My whole life was in limbo, but everything was looking good. I was getting in football shape, and my workout numbers were off the charts for speed, strength, and agility. In head-to-head tests, I was blowing NFL players away, and I was getting noticed.

I was right on track for my pro-day, where teams were scheduled to come in and watch me work out. I planned to finish my six-week program, do my pro-day, then fly home and see my daughter. Everything was going great—until April 19, 2004.

I had left my motorcycle in my buddy "Crazy's" custom bike shop in Minneapolis. It was a Harley chopper, and he was tricking it out and making it into one badass bike. I was getting it all beefed up. I must have put $70,000 into that machine.

When I got home, it started out to be a great day. Mya was with me, and I was playing with her on the couch. My old college roommate, Jesse Sabot, and his brother were visiting, and my brother was staying in my basement. I liked having all these good people around me.

Then I decided to go pick up my bike and see what Crazy had done to it. I was blown away. I was the King of the Road on that thing.

I ripped out of Crazy's parking lot on the edge of downtown Minneapolis, and headed home. My whole agenda for the weekend was to relax, recover from the training week, and spend time with Mya. A nice bike ride on a beautiful day seemed like the perfect prescription for me.

Jesse and his brother, my brother, and the rest of the crew had all come down to see the bike, and they were following me home. When I was showing off as we left the parking lot, the rear tire kicked out on me, and I realized this bike had some serious juice to it.

I blew through the intersection, and saw the light at the next turning from red to green as I sped down the street. Up ahead I see this car, and it looked like it was going straight, and there was a van ahead of the car pulling over into the turn lane in front of me. I planned to get behind the van and make the same turn. But then, all of a sudden, the woman driving the minivan who almost killed me decided she was going to cut me off and beat me to the turn, which left me nowhere to go. She was right beside me and moving closer, the van was in front of me blocking the turn lane, there was traffic coming toward me from the other direction, and there was traffic behind me. I had nowhere to go, and when I hit the brakes, it didn't do much good. It all seemed like it was happening in slow motion. I was going forty-five in a twenty-five. By the time I hit the van, I had only slowed to thirty-nine miles an hour.

I went face-first into that minivan, then up and over the top. My bike went underneath. Torn into three pieces.

After I landed on the street and stopped rolling, I jumped up to my feet and ran to the sidewalk. I was full of adrenaline, and was thinking that I had got really lucky. I remember feeling a sharp pain in my abdomen area when I hit the van, but I had no idea my jaw was broken, along with eight bones in my left hand. I also didn't know that the sharp pain I felt was my groin muscles being ripped from the bone. The pain didn't start to set in until the ambulance and the cops showed up. I figured out later that the handlebars of my motorcycle had gone right into my pubic bone at thirty-nine miles an hour.

My brother was telling the EMTs, "He's fine, everything's okay!," but as soon as I sat down, I figured out I had not only totaled my bike, but had wrecked my body, too. Still, I didn't want to get in the ambulance to go to the hospital, so Jesse drove me.

They told me at the hospital I didn't have any internal bleeding, but they ran down the list of injuries I did have. Broken jaw. Broken left hand. Bruised pelvis. Pulled my groin so severely, it's painful for me to even list it here six years later. I had just gone through six or seven weeks at Athlete's Performance to get into top physical condition. I was 298 pounds, doing high-impact weight training. I pissed it all away in about three seconds.

The first call I made was to Luke, and then to my football agent.

The only thing that held me together through that crash was the fact my body was rigid as hell. That weight training I had done with Luke saved my life. I could still talk because even though I broke my jaw, I refused to have it wired shut. My hand was in a small cast, which would stop my progress somewhat, but the worst thing was my groin injury. That was going to take forever to heal. There is no cast for that, no quick fix.

If I had any hope of making an NFL roster, and more importantly, if I was going to escape WWE, I knew there was only one choice. Injuries or not, I had to train.

I was pretty happy with my progress in the gym before the crash. I was bench-pressing 405, sets of eight; safety-squatting 860 pounds; and even though I weighed almost three hundred pounds, I was running a 4.67-second forty-yard dash. That was nearly running-back speed. I had NFL scouts interested in me.

But now, with my pro-day only two weeks away, I was all busted up. I was thinking maybe God wanted me to slow my ass down. I had just left pro wrestling, which I thought was smart; but then I jumped on my chopper and took off like there was no tomorrow, which was really a dumb-ass thing for me to do. Yes, I wanted to be a football player. First, though, I needed to get everything in perspective. It was a time for me to be looking at the more important things in life.

I went back to Phoenix and started recovery training. Lots of rehab—massage work, lifting weights, all sorts of exercises.

I couldn't do any directional movement, because I could hardly walk due to how badly my groin was pulled. I was in so much pain at the time that I couldn't even run in a straight line. No pro-day for me.

Three weeks went by, and my times and weight numbers were picking up, although my groin was healing a lot slower than I would have liked. But just when I was starting to think I had missed my shot at football, the Minnesota Vikings called. They wanted me to come up and work out for them. There was no way I was going to pass up this chance.

I was up front with the Vikings, and told them about my accident. When I worked out for them, they knew I could have done much better if I hadn't been hurt, and they decided to give me another month to heal, and then they were going to look at me again right before training camp. My injuries were so severe that there was no way I was going to get through an eight-week NFL training camp, but Luke really helped me get back into the best shape I could be in, all things considered.

Once I got to the training camp, it was right back to the Vicodin and anti-inflammatories. I'm not proud of it, but it's true, and I'm not going to sugarcoat or bullshit anyone in this book. I got through that training camp, and I was probably three-quarters of the man I should've been and maybe even less than that. Maybe I was only half the man I should have or could have been—but I was still the last guy cut from the squad.

I was proud of myself. There were guys who trained their whole lives to get to the NFL, and who were superstars for major college football teams, and they got cut. I played a little high school football, jumped on and off the WWE train, worked out with Luke for a few weeks, crashed my bike, busted myself up pretty good, and almost made it.

I know some people didn't believe me at the time, but getting cut wasn't a huge deal for me. I never thought of myself as a football player. I was just trying to do anything but pro wrestling. I just wanted to change everything about my life. I went pretty damn far during my little flirtation with the NFL, but when it didn't work out for me, I had to come to grips with the fact that I was unemployed, and I had a noncompete agreement that said I couldn't earn a living by being associated with, or appearing for, any wrestling or fighting organization in the world. Except, of course, the one owned by Vince McMahon.

I swallowed my pride, and had David Olsen get in touch with WWE for me. They said that Vince didn't want me back.

THE SWORD

ALL OF A SUDDEN my problems were mounting. I missed the NFL by an inch. IRS problems. A legal battle over my visitation rights regarding my daughter, Mya. No money coming in, and not that many options left because I signed that stupid noncompete clause with WWE. I had no one to blame but myself. My lawyers warned me not to sign that noncompete agreement, but I was in such a rush to get out of there, I got impatient and put my signature on that piece of paper.

That cost me a lot of time and money. I guess this is where I'm supposed to say "you live and learn," but it still burns me to this day how much money I lost because they knew I was miserable and wanted to break away from their company.

With all these pressures piling up, one on top of the other, I was depressed. Every day, I was drinking more and more vodka, chasing down more and more Vicodins. This was exactly where I was in WWE, except now I wasn't pulling in big money anymore. I was quickly burning through what money I had, and I had no clue what I was going to do next. I had walked away from my wrestling career, so that door was shut. Thanks to the noncompete clause, so was every other door, too.

I was angry. I was drunk. I was pilled up. I was going to do damage to someone or something. My first victim? Myself!

I ended up at a biker bar in Phoenix, right next door to which—and this may come as a big shock to you—there just so happened to be a tattoo parlor. I felt like life was holding a sword right up against my throat, so I went under the ink gun because I never wanted to forget exactly how I felt at that time.

The bad times only make you appreciate the good times even more, and if I was ever told that I could only keep one tattoo, this one of the sword pointing right up against my throat is the one I'd keep. I wouldn't even have to think about the answer. This tattoo on my chest has so much meaning to me. In some ways, it's funny, because the period of my life that I'm talking about is a time I so want to forget, but I know I can use this memory as motivation. And just in case I ever start slipping up, I have this sword right across my torso as a constant reminder of all the things that changed my life.

I look at that sword almost like it was a family crest. It's my inspiration to fight back, because if there's one thing I know deep in my heart about myself, it's that I am not a quitter. I am a warrior, and I will never let anything or anyone—be it the NFL or Vince McMahon—keep me down!

"RENA, WILL YOU MARRY ME?"

EVERYWHERE I LOOKED, all I could see was uncertainty. But there was one thing I was sure of: I wanted to marry Rena. However, before I could do this, I needed her to get out of WWE. "If we want a relationship," I told her, "neither one of us can work for that company. We both know the long-term side effects of everything there."

That was my only demand. Nothing else. Just that.

And so she left World Wrestling Entertainment. She had worked so hard to get back into that company, and now she was leaving it again, except this time she was giving up her career for me. It couldn't have been an easy decision. I was all stressed out, my future was up in the air, and my daughter was still very young. Like all couples, we had some differences to work through, but Rena was willing to do whatever it would take to make things work. She deserves a lot of credit, because at that time, I was just creating controversy everywhere I turned.

One day, of course, I pushed things too far, and Rena decided that she'd had enough of my bullshit. She was smart enough to pack her bags and go back to her own house in Florida.

I knew she was the woman I was going to marry, and I also knew I'd screwed up by driving her away. I started calling her, but she wasn't going to make it easy for me. I guess I should have taken the hint after a week of her not taking my calls. As things turned out, I'm glad I didn't take the hint.

You can think whatever you want about this statement, but I never really chased anyone before. It just wasn't my style. Here I am, calling her constantly, and I'll be the first one to admit I'm begging her to talk to me.

By the time two weeks had gone by, I was beside myself. Rena wouldn't answer the phone, wouldn't return my calls. She was sending a message loud and clear. She wasn't playing hard to get; she was letting me know that she would devote her life to me, but I had to play by the rules with her.

I wanted her to know how serious I was about building a life together, so I hopped on a plane, and in a last-ditch effort to be with the woman I knew I should spend my life with, I headed down to Orlando.

I made one stop on the way to the airport. I went to a jewelry store and bought an engagement ring. This was going to be "all or nothing," and the stakes had never been higher.

I had been to Rena's house a bunch of times, but I never wrote down the address. I knew how to get there from the airport, but that didn't do me a lot of good.

I got into a taxicab, and right away I'm arguing with this stupid cabbie, because he keeps telling me he needs an address. "Don't worry about the address!" I kept telling him. "Just turn right, go down six lights . . ."

I had to force myself to calm down, because I was going to punch this guy's lights out. Finally, I just got out of his cab, and ended up in another taxi.

This jackass of a driver pulls the same shit with me as the first guy. "I need an address, I must know where I am going!" Well, I'm trying to tell the guy where he's going. "You go down this road, turn right ..."

I ended up getting out of that cab, too. I was running out of patience. I just wanted to get to Rena's house, see the woman I love, and get her to marry me. I can't even get there, because these damned taxi drivers are all assholes!

So I get into the third taxi of the day, and I tell the guy, "Listen, I'm having a bad day. I just need to go home. I don't even know my own address. I just know how to get there. Please, just take me where I want to go, okay?"

The taxi driver was either laughing at me, or scared out of his mind. Either way, he says to me, "Just guide me along."

I was so happy to hear him say that.

Of course, it's not over yet.

Rena lived in a gated community, and wouldn't you know it, the gate is closed when we get there. So I'm sitting there for over half an hour with the taxi driver, trying to figure out a way in, when lo and behold, another car pulls up. We went right in behind it, and after all this trouble, I finally get to Rena's house.

I was so ready to see her. I rang the doorbell. I'm standing there, preparing myself for whatever reaction she has when she opens that door. If she's happy to see me, I'm scooping her up in my arms. If she's pissed, I know I have to make good on my stupid mistakes. So, what's it going to be?

Well, I didn't find out right away, because Rena wasn't home. I'm standing there ringing the doorbell, and I know someone is going to notice me standing in front of her house and call the cops.

I can't just break down the door, because she has all this security. Plus, it would probably piss her off. So, I decide to try to get in from the back of the house. Here's this three-hundred-pound gorilla jumping the fence into the backyard, and it's not like I'm inconspicuous. I'm just hoping to God that maybe she left the window open or something like that. Of course, she didn't. Everything is all locked up.

I saw a neighbor standing by his garage, and I knew he had seen me around with Rena enough to know we were a couple. That was a lucky break for me, because the guy never got suspicious. I told him I was working in the backyard and needed a screwdriver. It was the best excuse I could come up with.

I used the screwdriver he loaned me to get into one of her sliding doors, and of course the alarm goes off as soon as I get into the house. I knew the pass code, so I shut off the alarm, and now I'm inside. I returned the screwdriver to the neighbor, brought in my bags, and started waiting. I was sure Rena wasn't out of town, because it was obvious that the house had been lived in. I figured she would come back, and we'd settle our problems.

Well, I sat around for a couple of hours, and she still wasn't home. I started calling her from my cell phone, which was a dumb-ass move because she hadn't taken my calls in over two weeks. I didn't want her to know where I was, so I just kept calling her from my cell phone, and not from her landline.

I'm sitting in her house, and I'm stewing. I couldn't wait any longer, so I picked up her house phone and dialed her cell. You can probably imagine what must have gone through her mind when she looked at her cell phone and saw her own number pop up on the caller ID.

She answered the phone, and me just being me, I just said, "Hey, how are you doing?"

Rena was pissed. "Brock, where are you calling me from?"

Of course, I was going for broke here, so I said, "Don't you recognize the number?"

She couldn't believe it. "You better not be at my house!"

I told her, "Well, I'm here, and I'll be here when you come home, because I'm waiting for you!"

Just to teach me a lesson, Rena took her own sweet-ass time getting home, making me wait and wait and wait. Once she got home, I knew she was as happy to see me as I was to see her—but I still walked around on pins and needles.

I ended up spending a week with Rena in Florida. When she took me to the airport, she came inside the terminal with me. It was right there, by the waterfall in the Orlando airport, that I asked her to marry me.

I don't think my wife has ever regretted saying yes. I can tell you, I've never regretted it for a single moment. We were meant to be together.

MY NOT-SO-SECRET
MEETING WITH VINCE

I **WAS THE** last man cut from the Vikings squad. My mission was never to pursue a career in the NFL, but to escape WWE. Once I got cut by the Vikings and left Phoenix, I spent about thirty days doing nothing but hunting and thinking about my future.

I had no interest in some of the weird offers that were coming in. Tabloid news shows want to pay me for my story? No thanks.

Stupid meathead movie roles? I think I'll pass on those, too.

Autograph-signing appearances in shopping malls? I'm sorry, that's just not my style. I have never been one to prostitute myself out for the quick buck.

I needed to find something I could be proud of doing, and enjoy the ride while it lasted. I wanted to do something my parents would approve of, something that would allow me to provide the things for my family that I always envisioned them having.

I couldn't figure out which way to turn, and then my lawyer, David Olsen, called me with some interesting news. David had been contacted by New Japan Pro Wrestling, the big group based out of Tokyo and run by Antonio and Simon Inoki. They were thinking about all the hype they could build around a shooter who'd become the youngest WWE champion in history, and were looking to cut a deal right away.

I had never thought about wrestling in Japan, or anywhere else for that matter, because WWE had me sign that noncompete agreement which said I could only wrestle for Vince, and I thought I was on the shelf until 2010. So, instead of having David get back to the Inokis right away, I told him to contact WWE.

If I went back to the company, though, I didn't want it to be like the first time. I wanted to have some control over when and where I worked. I was going to make sure up front that I had time off written into my deal, and I wanted to get paid what I thought I was worth.

Over the next several months, David went back and forth with the WWE lawyers trying to work out the details. Finally, a one-on-one, supposedly secret, meeting between Vince and me was arranged.

This part still makes me laugh to this day.

As soon as I walked into the WWE offices, they had cameras all over me. Before Vince and I even said hello to each other, the front page of their Web site had the headline "Brock Lesnar Meets with WWE!"

So on one side of the world, I'm walking into Vince McMahon's office to see if we can patch things up, put everything behind us, and do some business together again. On the other side of the planet, the Inokis were probably reading about my "secret meeting" with Vince, and could have been starting to think they are in a bidding war with WWE.

By putting our "secret" meeting on the Internet, Vince gave me all the leverage I needed to negotiate with the Inokis. He might as well have put a big red bow on this early Christmas present. The Inokis had put so much thought into bringing me in, it was now a matter of pride for them. They were willing to pay whatever it took to keep me from going back to WWE.

I didn't want to have to go all the way to Japan to make a living. If I could have had my way, I would have ended up back in WWE, but on my own terms. I walked into that meeting with Vince to give him first dibs on my services. All he had to do was be reasonable with me. If he wanted me back, he had that opportunity. If he didn't want me back, then I was just wasting my time so that Vince could look me in the eye and tell me how disappointed he was that I left. It was his decision, and it wasn't going to take long for me to find out which way the meeting was headed.

Vince invited John Laurinaitis to join us in the meeting. Laurinaitis had replaced Jim Ross as head of the talent relations department, and Vince wanted him to sit in with us while we talked things out. I'm not one to beat around the bush, so I told Vince . . . right in front of John . . . that we were getting started on the wrong foot.

"I thought this was going to be mano a mano," I told Vince. Obviously, he had other ideas.

"Well, Brock," Vince said, setting the tone for the entire meeting, "John runs talent relations, and I would be disrespecting him if I asked him to leave this meeting. I'd be excusing him from a meeting that affects his entire department."

All I could think of was, "Just get to the part about my deal. I'm not even here ten minutes, and I'm already sour on the experience!"

Before we could talk about money, Vince and John had to play their little games with me. John started talking about the tattoo on my chest, and actually asked me to take my shirt off.

Right there. In the middle of a business meeting. And not just any business meeting, either, but one where the people involved were trying to put a lot of bad blood behind them. There were issues that had had a lot of time to work themselves out, but both sides were still hot at each other. We're trying to find a way to work together again, to make money with each other, and the head of the talent department wants me to take my damned shirt off in the chairman's office so I can show off my new tattoo?

Screw that.

That's when Vince stakes out his position, and tells me I'll have to start all over again because I walked out on my first deal. "Start at the bottom, and work your way back up to the top!" he tells me. "That's the only way this is going to work!"

Vince wasn't talking about a push. He was talking payroll. I'd have to come back for a deal worth a lot less than I had been making. The fact that I'd left on top meant nothing. Vince was offering me a rookie deal, and he knew it was a complete insult.

It didn't matter that my value was still high, that I put over Eddie Guerrero for the title and Goldberg at *WrestleMania*. It didn't matter that I could be back on top in no time at all, or that I could be back drawing Vince big money with the right reintroduction, the right angle, even just the right promo.

Vince wanted to bully me like he does everyone else, because most people who end up on the outs with Vince McMahon don't have a pot to piss in. They have to crawl back on their hands and knees, begging for scraps.

Well, I had a ton of problems and a tattoo that symbolized the sword I felt I had at my throat, but I wasn't going to let anyone talk to me like I'm a piece of shit. Vince was talking to me like I was some low-life jerk-off who had nowhere else to go.

What Vince never understood about me is that I am, at heart, still a poor kid from that farm in Webster, South Dakota. Yes, I lived the life of a rock star for a few years in WWE, but I knew I could be happy with my future wife no matter what I did for a living or how much money I made.

If I had to farm for a living, I'd be one happy, hardworking farmer, married to the woman I love, and satisfied with myself because I never let anyone talk to me the way Vince did in that meeting. He could have had me back, almost one hundred percent on his terms, except with just a little concession about the schedule, and he blew it.

After I walked out of my "secret" meeting with Vince that day, I headed for the airport. Rena asked me on the phone what had happened, and I told her the meeting went well. I also told her that I had swallowed my pride, and it looked like I was going to go back to work for Vince. But before I made the final decision, I wanted to see the contract his lawyers were supposed to send to David Olsen. When we got Vince's deal in writing, it still looked to me like a rookie deal, for rookie money, with no more days off than I had before. That was the moment I decided I was going to find out what the Inokis were willing to pay me to wrestle in Japan.

Brad Rheingans had been working with New Japan for about nineteen years, so I made sure I got him in on the deal. With Brad on my team, I had the perfect person to smarten me up to the Inokis' way of doing business. I knew going to Japan could be a big score, but I also knew I was going to have to have a good strategy to get that kind of money out of the Inokis.

I also guessed that Vince McMahon was going to do everything in his power to stop me from making a living.

BROCK LESNAR VS. WWE

IN JANUARY 2005, about nine months after leaving WWE, I went to Japan with Rena and Brad. I wanted to see exactly what opportunities I had waiting for me over there, but I had to be very careful not to do anything that would get me sued by Vince McMahon.

My lawyers and I decided it was best for me to pay for my own plane ticket, and sit in the front row. Did I know that this would only drive my price up with New Japan? Of course I did. My mission was to see what kind of show they put on, and how I could see myself making a big impact.

Once I got to Tokyo, the Inokis wanted to get every bit of publicity out of my arrival that they could. It was an interesting game. They were getting press based on me coming over to see their show, and I was becoming more and more valuable because I had not committed to them . . . or even to myself, really . . . that I was going to be a part of New Japan Pro Wrestling.

When I arrived at the arena, the Inokis kept pushing for more and more. They wanted to get as much out of me as they could. They asked if they could introduce me to the crowd. I didn't have one of my lawyers with me, but how could being introduced to the crowd hurt? I wasn't getting paid to be there. Yes, I was playing my cards, driving up my price, seeing what buzz I could manufacture before having to make some tough decisions. I'm in Tokyo. I'm not wrestling. I'm not performing. I'm sitting in the crowd, and I am going to be introduced as a celebrity in attendance.

The Inokis suggested that I walk down the big entrance ramp into the arena so the crowd could see me come in, and then be seated. They told me this is what they would do with any big celebrity guest.

The news hit the Internet within a matter of minutes. "Brock Lesnar Introduced at New Japan Show."

And then all hell broke loose.

WWE's lawyers were making all kinds of noise about my trip. Vince didn't want me having anything to do with any other wrestling organization, and the lawyers were making threats about enforcing my noncompete agreement and suing New Japan, too.

Vince didn't want me back unless I agreed to go right back to life on the road, with no breaks. That's what drove me away the first time.

But now, if I returned to WWE, I'd have to try to survive that schedule, and not even for the pay I had worked my ass off for that company to earn. No, Vince wanted me to come in and work that brutal, killer schedule for little to no money at all.

WWE'S lawyers were threatening to sue me if I even thought about working for any other wrestling company, anywhere in the world, in any capacity. The sword was at my throat. Anyone who knows me will tell you that I'm not one to back down from a fight. I wanted to work, and Vince was telling me I couldn't.

My lawyers were telling me that the noncompete agreement was unenforceable, for far too many reasons than I will bore you with here. You can't keep a human being from earning a living, and that's exactly the prison Vince McMahon and his team of attorneys was forcing me to live in. If I decided to work for New Japan, I could expect to get sued by WWE. If I wrestled a damn polar bear on the North Pole, WWE would sue me, if for no other reason than because they could. They love to bully people around that way.

This was a fight, so I decided to strike first.

I filed a lawsuit against World Wrestling Entertainment and asked the federal court in Connecticut to declare my noncompete clause illegal.

Anyone who knows Vince will tell you he loves a good fight, and he wasn't going to back down from this one. His lawyers countersued me for breach of contract, and wanted me to pay for all the damage I had caused WWE by leaving the company. They wanted me to pay for all their legal fees (I had enough of my own legal fees to pay, thank you) and asked the judge to declare the noncompete agreement to be binding. They wanted to force me to sit out the prime of my career, all the way until 2010, or go back to work for WWE.

Vince loves to tell everyone how much he hates managers, agents, and especially lawyers, but he plays the attorney game better than anyone. I had to pay my lawyers in Minnesota, and also a law firm on the East Coast that was licensed in the state of Connecticut. It looked to me like WWE's strategy was to make me go broke. Request more documents. Another extension of time. Another request for more paperwork. If they could spend me into a hole, I'd have to drop my lawsuit and come back on my hands and my knees, begging for forgiveness.

It was a smart strategy on Vince's part. Hey, just the cost of living was hard enough to manage, but I was funding a lawsuit for my freedom. I knew I couldn't back down, but paying all these legal fees was bleeding me dry.

I told my lawyers to cut a deal for me with New Japan, but the Inokis were leery of getting sued by WWE.

Oh, did I forget to tell you that WWE stopped all my royalty payments when they decided to sue me?

I had no income, and everyone was scared of the big bad monster WWE and their legal tactics. I can see how Vince beats all these other guys into submission. He almost did it to me.

I had to think long and hard about what to do next. Do I just cave in, suck it up, do what I have to do to make a living? Do I keep fighting this uphill battle, where I have to pay two sets of lawyers, against a company that appears to be intentionally running up my legal tab as a defensive strategy?

It took me a little while, but I finally made the decision to keep fighting. I could never look at myself in the mirror if I just tucked my tail between my legs and put up with the way WWE was trying to treat me. I had my lawyers finalize my deal with New Japan so I could have a few bucks to live on while I spent everything else on the lawsuit.

When I cut my deal with New Japan, I made sure to get Brad Rheingans in on it, because I wanted to use his experience with New Japan's management to my advantage, and keep him by my side in all my dealings. Plus, I figured going to Japan would be a great experience. I'd pick up some excellent coin, eat some fresh sushi, have some good times with Brad, and deliver a great big "screw you" to Vince.

That's how I entered the world of Japanese professional wrestling.

NEW JAPAN PRO WRESTLING

MY FIRST MATCH in Japan was a Triple Threat Match against Fujita and Chono on October 8, 2005. It really didn't matter who they put in the ring with me: I knew the Japanese crowds were looking for a monster heel. They wanted someone they could "ooh" and "aah" about, and I was going to be that guy. I was happy to be working and making money again, but my whole time there, I was waiting for bad news to drop at any moment. That's the mind game a lawsuit plays with you.

As soon as New Japan started advertising my first match, the WWE lawyers tried to stop me from appearing. They threatened New Japan, and claimed they were going to get an injunction to prevent me from doing the match. Right up until the time I stepped on the plane to Japan, I was actually expecting my lawyers to call me on my cell and say, "Go back home, Brock, WWE pulled such-and-such legal maneuver, and the match is off."

Lucky for me, WWE's lawyers were full of shit. WWE never sued New Japan, and they never got an injunction to prevent me from working my scheduled match. But that wasn't the end of the hassle.

I was scheduled to wrestle on a couple of shows in Japan in December, and then go back to work their big annual show on January 4, 2006. I thought all of the shows would go off without a hitch, because while the WWE's legal dogs had barked a lot, they had shown themselves to have no bite. They made all these threats about forcing me to sit out the October show, and they kept backing down every time. I thought it was a case of the Boy Who Cried Wolf.

I was wrong.

Right before I headed out to Japan for the December shows, WWE filed what is called a Motion for Temporary Restraining Order, or a "TRO." I wasn't too well versed in these legal terms at the time, but I've sure learned them thanks to my "hard-way education" from World Wrestling Entertainment and their team of attorneys. WWE asked the judge who was presiding over our lawsuit to issue an immediate injunction against me that would prevent me from wrestling on the New Japan shows. If I decided to ignore the TRO, I would be in contempt of court.

My lawyers fought back, but the judge was taking his time in making a decision. You can't tell a judge to hurry up "because Brock wants to know whether to get on the plane to Japan or not," so during my whole flight over to Japan, I'm wondering if I'm even going to get to work when I land. I kept thinking how pissed off I was going to be if I had to turn right back around once I landed in Japan because the judge ruled against me and in favor of WWE.

The judge, however, never granted the TRO, and I wrestled on . . . and got paid for . . . the December shows. When I got back to the United States, I was told that WWE "formally withdrew" its motion, because they knew it was a loser. They never really wanted the judge to make a decision. In my opinion, WWE's motion, like most of their threats, was just a legal form of harassment intended to make me lose sleep and spend as much money as possible on lawyers. I went back to Japan again for their major annual show on January 4, 2006, and did a few more shows after that. I'm sure it burned Vince's ass that he couldn't do anything to stop me.

I was a vengeful person for many years. "An eye for an eye" wasn't just a saying to me: it was a way of life. In time, I've come to learn just how much this kind of negativity wears you down, but back then I wasn't ready to accept that truth. My finishing maneuver in New Japan was the very same one I used in WWE.

In WWE, it was called the F-5. In New Japan, it was called "The Verdict."

That was my way of sending a message to Vince and his geek squad lawyers.

I planned on kicking WWE's ass in court, and I wanted the world to know I was still a top dog whose bite was every bit as bad as his bark, if not badder. Once the Inokis realized that Vince was not going to be able to stop me from wrestling for them, they went ahead and built their company around me. We were off to the races, and before anyone knew it, I beat Fujita and Chono in a Triple Threat Match to win the IWGP World Heavyweight Title.

One of my old coaches used to tell me that 80 percent of the things we spend our time worrying and having nightmares about never actually happen. We spend so much of our lives racking our brains about things that will never materialize. It's all such a waste of valuable time, but I'll be the first to admit I didn't understand this until I got into UFC and focused on the truly important things in life. Back when I had to travel all the way to Japan just to earn a living, the sword was still at my throat, and it was tough to have a positive outlook on anything.

With all that negativity around me, it didn't take long for me to get back on that vodka-and-Vicodin kick. Brad called me the other day to ask about this book, and he was reminding me of a match I had with a Japanese wrestler named Nakanishi. Brad thought it was one of the best matches he ever saw me fight, and we both remembered that I was half shooting on the poor guy. Unfortunately, that's all I remember about the match. Brad remembers so much more about it, but when you're poisoning your system with pills and alcohol, your memory is one of the first things that gets affected.

I can come up with a lot of reasons why I got back on that drugs-and-booze train again, but they're all excuses. My back was killing me at the time, and I was in constant pain. I went into the hospital for an MRI and found out I had ruptured two vertebrae, which meant I was flying across the world to wrestle with a broken back. The doctors were telling me my situation was serious enough that they were strongly recommending surgery. No thanks. Not for me. I knew too many athletes who had back surgeries, and never recovered. I was going to get through it on my own. But that's a lot easier said than done!

I was having what is called "strong style" matches against all the top guys New Japan had to offer. In WWE, everyone performs a very "safe" style, or as safe as professional wrestling can be, given that the company is built on the name "Entertainment." In New Japan Pro Wrestling, the wrestlers go out of their way to try to convince the audience that pro wrestling is still somewhat for real. The office actually encourages the wrestlers to go out there and beat the hell out of each other. If someone gets hurt, it's considered "good for the business."

I didn't mind wrestling "strong style," but doing it with two ruptured vertebrae was just plain stupid of me. I'd get back into my locker room with Brad and just collapse from the pain. I wasn't about to let anyone know how I was really feeling, so the only way to mask it all was to swallow more Vicodins and wash them down with more vodka.

I'm so blessed that I'm alive to tell this story, because there are a lot of people who went through the same thing as me who aren't around today.

Thank God I woke up one morning and decided that enough was enough. I knew if I kept on living this way, I would one day just stop living. Eventually, the odds catch up to you. There's no escaping the inevitability that something will go wrong. Whether it's choking on your own vomit while you're sleeping, or falling down when you're all messed up and smashing your head, there's too many ways to screw up when you've dulled your own senses to the point that you're numb to everything.

So I just stopped, cold turkey. I didn't stop because I went to some WWE-sponsored rehab. I didn't stop because I went into therapy, or counseling, or anything like that. I stopped because I wanted to see my daughter, Mya, grow up, and I knew I wasn't going to be there for her if I kept going in the wrong direction.

My timing couldn't have been better. The Inokis were having a lot of internal problems with their company, and I knew that New Japan was on a downswing. My time in their organization was quickly coming to an end, but I wanted to go out with a bang. That's where Akebono comes into the picture.

Akebono was a big-time national superstar in Japan. Even though he was originally from Hawaii and not Japan, he was respected as a legitimate sports icon, a folk hero, because he was a dominant Japanese sumo champion. I was happy when the Inokis told me they wanted me to do a match with him, because I knew we could build it up as the great big American heel champion against the even bigger Japanese sumo legend. I saw big dollar signs in that matchup.

Akebono is another giant of a man who has a great big heart. I believe we could have drawn big money against each other if the Inokis had played their cards right. I called Akebono "Big Chad," and he was one of the few guys in the wrestling business I considered to be a friend. I wanted to make our matchup mean something so that we could enjoy a long program and make a lot of money with each other.

But the Inokis had no long-term vision for Brock Lesnar vs. Akebono. They wanted me to beat him, right on television. I couldn't believe it. Why would they want me to kill what could be a great feud with one match on free TV?

Now I understood one of the reasons why Steve Austin had been so angry that day in Atlanta when WWE wanted to hotshot our first match on *Monday Night Raw*.

Because I'm a stubborn bastard, I demanded that we do what's called a "fuck finish," so we could come back with a rematch down the road. I had this idea about me and Big Chad doing all these big-man spots, and at the right time I'd smack him in the head with the IWGP title belt. The Inokis kept wanting me to just beat Big Chad, but I wore them down until they agreed to do the finish my way.

So Big Chad and I go out to the ring, and we're doing all the typical spots big powerful guys do against each other. We do the shoulder tackle attempts where no one budges, the spot where I run into the ropes and collide with Big Chad, or he comes charging into me and we both end up in each other's faces.

When it came time for the finish, I cracked him upside his big melon head with the title belt just like I planned. Big Chad dropped to the canvas, I covered him, and the entire arena went quiet. Dead silence. Not a single sound from the crowd. The audience wasn't buying it. They didn't pay to see a "fuck finish," and they're too intelligent to buy into a cheap horseshit heel victory like that. What a dumb-ass mistake I had just made!

The referee dropped down and started counting, and I'm saying to Big Chad, "Kick out, you son of a bitch, kick out." One . . . two . . . and the instant before the referee hits the canvas for the three count, Big Chad gets his arm up in the air, and the people went nuts.

We ended up doing some ridiculous finish that served no purpose except to piss off the Inokis, but at least Big Chad cared enough to give them the best match we could manage, and I think, all things considered, it was one hell of a match.

The fact that Big Chad and I could put together a solid match didn't surprise me. He's a trained athlete with a lot of pride, and so am I. What did surprise me was that the Inokis didn't try to get me to drop the title before I left Japan. They probably knew better than to make me feel like I was being backed into a corner, because I was already pissed off that they started playing games with my money.

I thought I was being smart when I went to Japan, because I insisted on private transportation, first-class hotel accommodations with all expenses paid, you name it. If I have to travel halfway around the world to work, at least I'm going to be comfortable while I'm over there.

Part of my deal with New Japan was also to get paid up front. My lawyers set up an escrow account in the United States, and our deal was that I don't get on a plane until the Inokis wire my money into that account. Then, when my match is over, the money is released directly to me so I never have to worry about going over to Japan and getting stiffed on my payoff. The system worked . . . for a while.

On one of my last trips to Japan, I didn't get all my money up front, but I got on the plane anyway. I figured the Inokis needed me because I was their champion, and I wasn't going to step into their ring until I got the word that all of my money had been deposited into the U.S. account. What could go wrong?

Plenty. But I should have known that. Another lesson in life. And, I guess, an interesting story for this book.

When my match was over, the Inokis threw me onto the bus with all the other boys headed to the airport. What the hell? It was in my contract that I was supposed to have a car and driver from the time I land in Japan until the time I'm dropped off at the airport to go home. That bus ride is just brutal, and I wanted no part of it.

The Inokis knew I wasn't expecting to end up riding the bus, and I kept wondering to myself why they would give the IWGP World Heavyweight Champion such a bush-league send-off.

What game were they trying to play with me?

I had been schooled on all sorts of shenanigans the Inokis could try and pull on me. Brad had smartened me up to a famous negotiating trick the Inokis liked to use. They take you to lunch or dinner, and then just stare at you, trying to make you feel uncomfortable. They want you to do all the talking so that you reveal your cards and expose your own business strategy. The first three times I met with the Inokis, that's exactly how they tried to play me.

Thanks to Brad, I was wise to that tactic, so it didn't work with me. I would stare back at the Inokis, and talk about whatever popped into my head. I'd keep saying things like, "How about this weather?"; "This food is really great"; "What a beautiful country you have." I would go on about anything and everything . . . except business. I knew their game, and I was ready for it. That probably drove them crazy.

Another game I was ready for was the Inoki Slap. I guess part of the initiation over in Japan is that all the newcomers end up getting slapped by Antonio Inoki, who is a living legend over there. I let them know where I stood on that one right away. No one was going to slap me. Not Inoki. Not anyone. They got the point.

But when they threw me on the bus with everyone else, I looked over at Brad, who had seen it all in Japan. Even he didn't know what was coming next, so we knew to be prepared for anything.

When we got to the airport, Simon Inoki comes up to me and says in this soft-spoken, respectful tone, "Mr. Lesnar, you should leave the title belt with me, because we want to polish it up for you and fix the rhinestones so that the belt looks very nice for when you come back to Japan!"

The Inokis had to know there was a chance I wasn't coming

back, so that meant there was a possibility they were going to ask me to turn over the title belt. I was one up on them, though, because I had the title belt buried all the way at the bottom of my suitcase … and you can just imagine what my grip on that suitcase must have been like. I was holding on for dear life, because they still hadn't paid me, and I wanted to keep their title belt as an insurance policy. As long as I had possession of the IWGP Heavyweight Championship belt, I knew they would find a way to come up with the money they owed me.

As polite as Simon was to me, I was even more polite to him. I thanked him for the offer to take care of the belt for me, but told him that I was planning on polishing it myself back home, and that I was going to make the rhinestones look nice for the New Japan fans.

Always trying to stay one step ahead of everyone, the Inokis must have anticipated my response, because Simon had a couple of the New Japan wrestlers with him. It looked to me and Brad like they were going to try to strong-arm me for the title belt. They had the advantage because I was a foreigner on their home turf and didn't speak the language, and if security jumped in they could say anything they wanted to. But, when those guys tried to intimidate us, Brad and I stared right back at them as we backed ten steps to the ticket counter, where I just let them know in no uncertain terms, "I'm taking the title with me!"

There was nothing they could do at that point unless they wanted to create a major incident in an international airport, so Brad and I checked in and got on the plane with the title belt still in my possession. I had heard New Japan was talking to TNA about a joint promotion, and it was easy to figure out that they were going to want me to come back and drop the title. That gave me a lot of negotiating leverage. I had something they wanted, and they had the money to pay me, so I used that to my advantage.

It wasn't long before Simon Inoki called my lawyers and wanted to set up a big title match in Japan. I told my lawyers, "Here's my price, give them the number and tell them to take it or leave it." They tried to counter, so we didn't have a deal.

As the months rolled by, Simon kept calling, but he wouldn't meet my price. Eventually, over a year later, after I was well into training for my first MMA fight and had more or less put wrestling in my past (although the IWGP belt looked good hanging in my garage), my lawyers got a another call from Simon. The Inokis had cut ties with New Japan and were starting a new promotion called "IGF." They needed a main event for their first show and they wanted it to be Brock Lesnar vs. Kurt Angle for the IWGP title. Now they were willing to meet my price.

I agreed to do it, but, since Kurt was working for TNA, I made Simon confirm that both TNA and Kurt were committed to the match, and let them know that it could not take place until after my first MMA fight.

I enjoyed getting back in the ring with Kurt for one night and had no problem dropping the title to him.

When I did that match, I was sure that I would never have to lace up a pair of wrestling boots again . . . with just one exception. In the back of my mind, I knew that when I became a big enough commodity doing something else in life, there would always be a big payday waiting for me when I decided to come back for one big event, one big night, one big match.

But that was looking far into the future.

Brock Lesnar vs. WWE.
WWE vs. Brock Lesnar.

Before I ever got to that last match with Kurt, I had spent a fortune fighting against a big, publicly traded company that had unlimited resources. WWE did an excellent job of making me spend a ridiculous amount of money fighting for the simple right to go out and work for a living, but the day of reckoning was at hand.

In February 2006, the judge ordered us to enter into what's called mediation, which is an attempt to settle the case before a trial, in front of a federal magistrate, in Bridgeport, Connecticut. If we were not able to reach a settlement, the judge would finally decide the motion I had filed nearly a year earlier to have my noncompete agreement declared to be a worthless piece of shit. WWE was running out of ways to delay that from happening, but what was I going to do once I was a free man?

The mediation was scheduled for the day after the Super Bowl, so David Olsen and I flew in and caught part of the game in the hotel bar. We got up the next morning and headed for the courthouse, and I wasn't holding out any hope that WWE would accept any settlement because Vince McMahon wasn't going to allow me to show that his noncompete agreements were unenforceable.

WWE claimed that my demand for freedom was outrageous. I thought WWE's offers were insulting. We kept going back and forth, and I just wanted to walk out and go home, but the judge had ordered us to hash things out this way, so we finally worked out the outline of a deal.

Settling the case was the right move to make, because if it came to trial, and even if I won in court, there would be appeals and more delays, and I just wanted to be done with it all and move on with everything. WWE was motivated to settle because they didn't want a public court declaring their noncompete clauses to be illegal. That would open the floodgates and cause them all sorts of problems with other wresters who might be thinking about leaving.

I've been warned by my lawyers that I can't go into detail here about the terms of the settlement because it's confidential. What horseshit. I made some compromises, and so did WWE. In the end, we both got a deal we could live with.

There. I didn't reveal any specifics, but you get the point. WWE didn't lose face, and I was a free man, with my whole life ahead of me, and the ability to choose how I wanted to earn a living so that I could feed my family. All I had to do now was make the decision regarding what I wanted to do.

I didn't have to think about it very long. I wanted to compete as a real athlete. I wanted to test myself. I talked it over with Rena, who was now my wife, and she assured me she would be supportive in anything I decided I was going to do. My wife knows I'm a competitor, and that competition is what drives me. It's in my blood. It's what I want to do. It's what I was made for.

In 2006, the fight business was picking up steam and getting a lot of serious attention from the media. It looked to me like there was money to be made if I could stir up some noise and grab everyone's attention again. I knew it wouldn't be easy, but nothing worthwhile in life ever is.

My legal battle with WWE was behind me. So was the NFL, and my dance with vodka and Vicodins, and, I thought, Japan Pro Wrestling. It was time to get back to doing what was second nature to me, what I had been trained to do since I was five years old.

So, looking for the next great challenge in my life, I got into the world of mixed martial arts. A whole new adventure was about to begin.

GETTING STARTED IN MIXED MARTIAL ARTS

WHEN I DECIDED to become a fighter, there were certain things I had to accept from day one. I'm an athlete and a wrestler, but that doesn't automatically make me a great mixed martial artist. To get to the top of the sport, I was going to need a lot of coaching.

I asked around about all the different training facilities, and decided to give Pat Miletich's gym in Bettendorf, Iowa, a try. Pat was one of the pioneers of mixed martial arts, and he is very well respected within the MMA community. He's a former UFC Champion, and his gym has produced guys like Matt Hughes, Tim Sylvia, Jens Pulver, and Robbie Lawler. I immediately liked Pat because he was originally an amateur wrestler, so he knew what it would take to transform another wrestler into a fighter.

I trained with Pat and his team for a while, and during the time I was with them I really learned a lot. This is no knock on Pat, because I respect his work and appreciate all that I learned from him, but I soon realized that his gym wasn't for me.

I figured I had money again, and I could afford to create my own camp, one that was dedicated to one and only one purpose, which was making me the best fighter I could be in the shortest period of time. I didn't want to spend years and years going through MMA's equivalent of my time in Louisville. I wanted to fight for a living, and my thought was that if you have a gym designed to accommodate a bunch of fighters, then no one gets the full benefit of the coaching staff. It's spread too thin. Where's the focus?

But if you have your own training facility, and everyone is dedicated to the goal of making you the best, you have a better chance of reaching your full potential. There's a lot of money at the end of that rainbow, and I wanted to reach for the pot of gold.

From the moment I decided to get into mixed martial arts, I knew I wanted to be in the UFC. That's the big league . . . the only place to be. The UFC is the most professionally run organization, and the people there have the resources to put on big-time fights for big-time money. No rinky-dink bush-league bullcrap for that organization. It's first class all the way.

The best thing about the fight business is that people pay to see a fight, and for the most part, you're going to see someone win and someone lose. It's a simple formula. If you want to be the best, you have to enter the fight and go for broke. No one is going to be champion for long by attempting to win on points.

Ultimately, there are only two positions a fighter can be in. Either you're number one, or you're not. For me, number one is the only place to be, because number two is just not good enough. It's the same as being last.

I had my goals set, but I also had a problem. The UFC saw me as a WWE "fake" wrestler. Yes, I had a name, but I had no MMA experience to speak of, which meant I had to start somewhere else. Believe it or not, that road led me right back to doing business with a company in Japan.

I was getting offers to fight as soon as word got out that I had been training at the Militech camp. It didn't matter if they promoted fights in arenas, on beaches, or in high school gyms, everyone wanted to promote my first mixed martial arts fight.

In April 2006, David Olsen and a new member of my legal team, Brian Stegeman, set up a meeting for me with the Japanese promotion K-1. This promotion is owned by a company called FEG, and they sent their international operations manager, Daisuke Teraguchi, and their Japanese-American lawyer, Toru Nakahara, to Minnesota to cut a deal with me.

We met at the Minneapolis Grand Hotel for a sushi dinner.

The food was great, but the meeting was going way too slow for my taste. Unlike the Inokis, who just sit there and stare at you, waiting for you to tip your hand, these guys just wanted to talk and talk and talk. I thought they would never get down to the bottom line, so against my lawyers' advice, I spoke up and cut to the chase. Right in the middle of the California rolls, I told them how much I needed for one fight or there was nothing further to talk about.

To their credit, Daisuke and Toru didn't even blink. They calmly asked if they could have a few minutes to discuss my demand in private. Feeling my oats, I generously said they could have fifteen minutes, and then I wanted an answer.

I went outside with David and Brian, and we just looked at one another. I was supposed to let them do the talking and negotiating, but I'd felt like the meeting was going nowhere with everyone just smiling at each other and telling stories. My lawyers were in disbelief, because by handling the meeting the way I'd done, they thought I might have killed my MMA career before it started, and I wasn't about to disagree. We started laughing, because depending on what happened in the next fifteen minutes, I was either going to fail Negotiating 101, or get an A-plus in the graduate-level course. And the suspense wasn't going to last very long.

David bet me the FEG execs would be sitting in a cab on their way to the airport by the time we returned. When we walked back into the restaurant, though, they were still sitting at the table. They told us they could probably make the deal work, but that they would need to confirm the details with some people in Japan before they could commit. The fact that they weren't already halfway back to Tokyo seemed like a very good sign.

While my lawyers were working out the details with K-1, I was working on becoming a fighter. Part of the agreement was that I could choose my own trainers, and FEG would foot the bill. They wanted me ready to fight by August 2006. There were a lot of rumors floating around that they were trying to get my first opponent to be Royce Gracie, UFC's very first star and the heir to the Brazilian jujitsu throne.

I was living just outside Minneapolis, and I was looking for a place to train locally. I didn't want to go to California or Nevada or anywhere else to train. As far as I was concerned, my traveling days were over.

Everyone I talked to on the local MMA scene seemed to have a high opinion of Greg Nelson, who ran the Minnesota Martial Arts Academy, so I stopped by his gym one day. Greg was a former U of M wrestler like me, had trained UFC World Champion Sean Sherk and others, and he agreed to take me on and get me ready for my K-1 fight.

Now that I was a professional fighter, and was about to make a lot of money, my lawyers told me they were creating a new company for carrying on my business as a fighter, and that I had to choose the name. David, Brian, and I were on a three-way phone conversation, and we were just throwing names back and forth.

The "Death Collector" had been suggested by a guy who wanted to do T-shirts for us, but that was too WWE for me. And then I said, what about "DeathClutch"? That name really worked for me, because after the lawsuit with Vince and all of the other shit that I had been through, I felt like I had been in one DeathClutch after another. I could hear the call of the match in my head: "Lesnar gets his hands around his opponent's body . . . it's the DeathClutch!"

I couldn't wait to get started, but just as I was ramping up my training, K-1 told me that they had not yet secured an opponent for what I thought would be my October 2006 fight. Oh, wait. It gets worse. They didn't have an arena, or even a pay-per-view clearance yet either. My goal was to be in a major-league organization, but I knew at that moment I was still in the minors.

K-1 offered me big money for an extension on my contract. If I told them no, I'd just have to take a fight for another minor-league organization before the UFC would seriously consider me.

Since I was already in business with K-1, I agreed to the extension, and kept training with Greg Nelson.

In the fall of 2006, I heard that K-1 had signed "The Techno Goliath," a seven-foot one-inch Korean kickboxer and MMA fighter named Hong-Man Choi, and wanted to pit us against each other in May 2007 at Dodger Stadium in L.A.

I never heard of Hong-Man Choi, so we looked him up. He was known for being this big entertaining son of a bitch, a friendly gentle giant who could maul people in fights. But the one thing that I couldn't get over was the size of his head. I mean, his noggin was enormous, even bigger than Big Show's. It was massive. I kept thinking that as soon as the referee said "fight," I was going straight for that huge target right between his shoulders. Hong-Man Choi had an international reputation, but he was big and slow, and I knew I could eat him up.

It was around this time that I talked to my old U of M wrestling coach, Marty Morgan. Since I was scheduled to fight a giant, I wanted to train with some big guys. Marty was training Cole Konrad at the University of Minnesota, and I started hitting the punching bag with Marty while rolling around with Cole and the other heavyweights on the squad.

I felt alive again. After all I had been through, it didn't matter who they put in front of me that first fight. I had a new lease on life, and I wasn't going to fail.

About a month before my scheduled fight, K-1 tells us there is going to be another delay. They couldn't get Dodger Stadium, so now the fight was going to be moved to June 2007 at the L.A. Coliseum. You know the routine. K-1 said they were planning to make this the biggest MMA fight ever, and that they were going to put a hundred thousand people in the stands. They expected all of L.A.'s Korea Town to show up for Big Head, and all of the WWE fans to show up for me.

I didn't want to hear the hype. I wanted to get started with my new career, and while I'm making sweet dough because of my contract with K-1, I knew I'd be spending my best fighting years dealing with delays and bullshit games. I simply want to train, fight, and make money. I don't want to have to worry about all the stuff the promotion is supposed to take care of. That's their job.

I know I'll live up to my end. You live up to yours.

Unfortunately, I never got the chance to knock Big Head out, because someone else beat me to it. About a month before our fight, the idiot did a K-1 kickboxing match in Japan, took a big shot to his big head, and went down like a felled tree. Scheduling him for an event so close to our fight was just plain stupid of K-1.

When Hong-Man Choi did the medical testing right before our fight, the California State Athletic Commission declared him unfit to compete.

K-1 offered me Min Soo Kim as a last-minute replacement. He was a South Korean fighter that had won an Olympic Silver Medal in judo. I didn't care who he was, or what he had won, I knew I was going to steamroll right over him.

I have to give it to K-1, they probably put fifty thousand or so people into the Coliseum on a beautiful June evening to watch me beat up Min Soo Kim. They also did their best to create a spectacle, including my grand entrance from the Olympic flame at the top of the stadium.

My job, to me, was easy. Wait for the referee to say "fight," and go right after Min Soo Kim. Poor bastard had no idea what he was in for. I took him right down and pounded him out. The fight lasted sixty-nine seconds, and I walked away without a scratch on me. Better yet, because the fight was delayed several times, each extension of my contract cost K-1 more money. All in all, I pocketed a lot of money for what turned out to be about a minute's worth of work in the ring.

This is the business for me!

GETTING DANA WHITE'S ATTENTION

IN WWE, YOU need to get Vince McMahon's attention. In the UFC, that man is Dana White.

I'm no fool. Beating up Min Soo Kim wasn't going to get me into the UFC. That organization was getting hotter and hotter, and mixed martial arts was finally being taken seriously by the mainstream sports media as a real sport. The last thing they needed was to give their critics ammunition by signing the big bad former WWE champion who'd had only one real fight, and that against a lower-tier opponent.

Kurt Angle and a bunch of other pro wrestlers were talking the talk, but no one was backing it up. I wanted to be the number one mixed martial arts fighter in the world. I wanted to be the champion. I wanted to main event the biggest pay-per-views, be the greatest heavyweight the sport had ever seen. But why would Dana White give a shit about me yet? I was just another guy making a lot of noise.

I had David Olsen and Brian Stegeman try to set up a meeting with the UFC, but I don't have patience for games and everyone trying to position themselves in a business negotiation. I like to get things done.

I've spent a good part of the last decade trying to avoid the media, but this was one time when being open to the press would be to my advantage. The UFC had a big fight coming up, with "Captain America" Randy Couture defending his title against Gabriel Gonzaga. What would happen if I just happened to show up? What would the UFC's reaction be if they knew I was coming?

I spent a couple thousand bucks to get the best tickets for me and my lawyers, and I had them leak to the press that I was going to be at the fight. I also did some radio shows where I let it slip that I would be in Vegas to watch Couture fight Gonzaga.

When I showed up for the fight, it was funny because there were a lot of celebrities in the crowd that night, and at one time or another every one of them was up on the big screen. Actors. Basketball players. Football players. Singers. Other fighters. But not me. Not even once.

MY LAWYERS BET me that the UFC would not put a camera anywhere near me, because I wasn't under contract to them, had just fought for a rival organization, and, most importantly, I was that guy from WWE. We knew the UFC didn't want anything to do with sports entertainment, because fans accepted the UFC as the real deal and there was no reason to toy with that perception.

I'm not saying the UFC did anything to make me feel unwelcome. I'm sure they were happy taking my money for the tickets. But they didn't do anything to make me feel welcome, either. When the show came to an end, the lights were coming up, the cameras were going down, the fans were leaving the building, and I had to make a quick decision.

That's when I said to my lawyers, "Boys, I'm hopping the rail, and no one better try and stop me." Lawyers being lawyers, they just started getting ready for any legal issues that might come about because of my move. Deep down, they loved the fact that their client had such balls.

I jumped down to the main floor, pushed my way through the crowd, and walked right past security. When I got near the Octagon I found myself directly behind Dana White, so I tapped him on the shoulder and introduced myself.

We found an empty room in the back of the arena, and Dana sat down with me and my lawyers. I'll give him credit; Dana didn't pull any punches. That's a good thing for a promoter in the real fight business. He came right out with it. "What makes you think you can do this, Brock? What makes you think you can be in the UFC with the best fighters in the word?"

I told Dana, "Don't look at me like I'm an entertainer thinking he's a real athlete. I AM A REAL ATHLETE, an NCAA Division I Heavyweight Champion. Pro wrestling just offered me a chance to get out of debt and make a lot of money right out of college."

I only had a few minutes to make my case because Dana had to get to the postfight press conference. I was just as up front with him as he was with me. I told Dana I don't have the time to work my way up in small organizations, fighting tomato cans. Either I can be a champion fighter, or I can't. I asked Dana to just give me one chance, with the best part of it being that the UFC couldn't lose in the deal.

If I win, the UFC has the golden goose. If I lose, someone else is going to become a star at my expense. Either way, my fight will draw money. MMA fans will pay to see me get my ass kicked. WWE fans will pay to see one of their own take on the best the UFC has to offer. There was no downside to the idea.

Dana knew this was a win-win proposition, but he also knew he had to throw me to the wolves. If Dana was going to give a WWE guy a shot, without ruining his own credibility, it couldn't look like a work or an easy setup. It had to be against a real opponent. There are no easy fights in the UFC, and Dana wasn't going to offer me one just to build me up. I wasn't looking for any favors, either. I wanted to start at the top.

Dana had to leave for the press conference, but I wanted an answer. I got the one I was looking for. The UFC was going to give me a shot.

At the time, the promotion was looking to do something with its former Heavyweight Champion Frank Mir, and I was the perfect answer to everyone's problems. Mir had been in a motorcycle accident that derailed his career, and he was in the process of making his comeback. He's a big guy, dangerous on his feet and on the ground. No one could call a fight with Frank Mir a setup.

It was a perfect scenario for Dana and the UFC. Either I was going to defeat a former Heavyweight Champion, and launch my own career from the top, or Frank was going to kick my ass and show the world that WWE guys have no business stepping into the Octagon.

When I got home I watched some tapes of Frank's past fights. He had good technical skills, and he was very capable, but I saw a guy who wasn't in my league.

Whether was or wasn't really didn't matter to me. I was getting one chance in the UFC, and I planned to rip out whatever heart Mir had and feed it right back to him. I was going to make a statement. And I was going to make a lot of money doing it.

The fight was set for *UFC 81* on February 2, 2008, at the Mandalay Bay Events Center in Las Vegas. Super Bowl weekend.

The UFC promoted the fight with everything they had. You couldn't walk down the street without seeing my face on a billboard or poster. I was all over the TV, radio, and the Internet. If you didn't know I was fighting that weekend, you just weren't paying attention.

It was a smart move on their part. A good investment. The UFC made money on me that day, and I think it's a safe bet to say they have continued to make money on me ever since.

But everyone knows what happened.

There's a saying about how sooner or later everyone loses in the UFC. I lost sooner.

I took Frank down right away, and was pounding him. The crowd was going crazy. The noise was deafening, and I couldn't hear the referee when he pulled me off Frank. For a minute, I thought the fight had been stopped and that I had won. But my hand wasn't getting raised; instead I was being led to my corner, and Frank was being given a moment to shake the cobwebs from his scrambled brain.

Referee Steve Mazzagatti said that I had illegally hit Frank in the back of the head when he was down. That was Mazzagatti's reason for standing us up. Frank was given some time to recover, but I immediately took him down again, and resumed beating his ass.

I had the fight won, but then I made a stupid rookie mistake. I was in too much of a hurry to finish the fight, and I stepped into Frank's legs when he was on the ground. I was trying to get a better position, where I could just crack him in the face and knock him out, but I fell right into the same trap I had been trained not to fall for. We must have practiced that scenario about a thousand times in training. I left myself open, and Frankie Boy rolled me right into the knee bar. I had no choice. Tap out, or let him break my leg. I tapped, and I have no one to blame but myself.

I know I handed Frank that victory. I gave it to him. He didn't deserve to win. He's not a better fighter than I am. On his best day, he's not half the athlete I am on my worst. I gave him my leg on a silver platter, just handed him that submission. That was my loss, not Frank's win. I screwed up.

I was a very lucky man that night, because I impressed enough people, especially Dana White, that I got to keep my job in the UFC. I think I'm the only guy in the history of the company that came in with no experience, got beat in ninety seconds, and was declared a hot prospect when it was over.

Still, that loss to Frank Mir chapped my ass real good.

I came from piss-poor South Dakota, and worked my way to become an NCAA Champion, and then Undisputed WWE champion. I could have played professional football if I wanted to spend a year in Europe to learn the game. When I'm almost thirty, I go into the mixed martial arts game, get a shot in the UFC, beat Frank's ass for a minute and a half, only to hand him a victory?

Just thinking about it now gets me pissed off all over again. I absolutely knew in my heart, my mind, and my soul that I am a better fighter than Frank Mir. Losing to Frank was one of the worst moments of my life, because I lost to someone who simply did not deserve to beat me, let alone even be in my Octagon.

I wanted a rematch!

I knew I'd have to work my way through some people to get back to Frank, but I didn't care who they put in front of me. I wanted Frank Mir again, and I wanted him in the worst way. Every thought I had about Frank was consumed with bad intentions.

GETTING BACK ON THE HORSE

UFC 87 WAS scheduled for August 9, 2008, at the Target Center in Minneapolis, the UFC's first-ever event in the state of Minnesota. I was going to fight in my adopted hometown, a couple of miles away from the U of M campus where I had wrestled for the Gophers.

I was originally matched up with UFC Hall of Famer Mark Coleman, who has a strong wrestling background and had had fights all over the world, but he suffered an injury shortly before the event and had to back out. With Coleman gone, the UFC asked me if I would fight "The Texas Crazy Horse," Heath Herring. I didn't even think about it before I said yes. I told Dana when we first met, I would fight anyone he wanted to throw at me, and I meant it. I wasn't interested in building a résumé littered with easy victories. I came to the UFC to fight, and I was willing to step into the Octagon with anyone.

Besides, I'm a businessman. There's a little bit of money on the undercard . . . but there's a whole lot of money at the top. Which one would you go for? My goal was never to be the third match on the card in WWE, and that's an environment in which the winners are predetermined. In the UFC, the outcomes are for real. You pit your athleticism and desire to succeed and win against the other trained athlete's desire to succeed and win. One man moves on, the other drops down one or two notches. Keep going up, reach the top, make the money.

And like Curt Hennig taught me, "Get in to get out."

I'm a big-money athlete. That's not my ego talking. It's a fact. That's how I view myself. If I thought of myself any differently, I wouldn't be a big-money athlete. I'd be some guy imagining what it would be like to be a main eventer. I dream, just like everyone else. I also go after my dreams and make them happen in reality.

Heath Herring was no slouch. He was a fighter with a tough guy's reputation that he earned by fighting top-level guys like Fedor, Nogueira, Kongo, Cro Cop, Belfort, and Kerr. Heath was 43–27–1 before our fight. That's a lot of experience in the fight game. This was a man who knew his way around every inch of that Octagon. For me, it was only my second fight in the UFC.

I don't think Heath took me seriously, and that rubbed me the wrong way. He looked at me like I was a greenhorn, a WWE wrestler who didn't belong in the Octagon with an experienced veteran like him. He acted as if it was beneath him to fight me, and I was determined to make him eat his own words. I'm sure to his friends and family, Heath is an "okay guy," but I just didn't like him.

I'm sure that Heath Herring doesn't like me, either . . . after all, I broke his face.

I never want to take away any man's ability to earn a living, but I have to admit I enjoyed that punch. One shot, and Herring was reeling backward, ass end over teakettle, with a broken orbital bone. If he hadn't been such a tough bastard, the fight would have been stopped right there. But for three rounds, no matter how much I beat his ass, he just kept coming back for more. Heath took that beating like a man, and he never even thought about quitting. I have to give him that. He at least earned that much.

I won a unanimous decision for my first victory in the UFC. Heath Herring has never fought again.

UFC 91: MY FIGHT VS. RANDY COUTURE

I **WAS TOLD** that my next UFC fight was going to be against Cheick Kongo, the French Muay Thai kickboxer. Kongo is one of the best strikers in the game, and I thought I would match up well with him because I could easily take him down and control him on the ground.

Then I got the word that Dana White wanted to offer me the opportunity of a lifetime. I wasn't going to fight Cheick Kongo. I was going to fight Randy Couture for the UFC Heavyweight Championship of the World.

Randy is the Godfather of MMA, a living, breathing legend who is still one tough old bastard. Randy was upset with the UFC when negotiations for a match with Fedor Emelianenko fell apart, and Randy's people told him he could "retire" from the UFC while he was still champion, and then go fight for another organization. From what I understand, the whole idea was for Randy to go elsewhere and get a piece of the action and a bigger payday. The UFC and Randy ended up exactly like me and WWE. Everyone was suing everyone else, which means a lot of time and money was being spent, with no return on that investment.

The UFC made the decision to create an "interim title," which I liked to call the "fake title," since to win that championship, all you had to do was beat another contender. If you want to rule over a kingdom, you have to dethrone the reigning king. Randy was the king of the heavyweight division, but the UFC had grown tired of waiting for him to defend his crown, so they wised up and decided to take a page right out of Vince McMahon's playbook and turn a bad situation into a moneymaker.

The plan was to first settle the lawsuit with Randy. The UFC's lawyers had him up against the cage, because there was no way he was going to be able to jump to another organization while he was still under contract to the UFC. No judge was going to buy the "retirement" ploy and then allow Randy to "come out of retirement" just so he could get a piece of his fight with Fedor.

As things stood now, Randy was going to defend the title against me. In the meantime, two other heavyweights would battle it out for the fake title . . . I mean the interim title . . . and then the two champions would meet for the Undisputed UFC Heavyweight Championship of the World. The decision was an example of marketing genius, a win-win for everybody.

Couture settled his lawsuit with the UFC and agreed to defend his title at *UFC 91* on November 15, 2008, at the MGM Grand Garden Arena in Las Vegas. I could not ask for a bigger or better opportunity in life.

A lot of hard-core UFC fans resented the fact that I was being given a title shot in only my third UFC fight, my fourth MMA fight overall, but my attitude was very simple.

Screw them.

Only a fool would turn down a chance to fight Randy Couture for the UFC Heavyweight Championship in Las Vegas. What was I supposed to do? Say "no thank you"?

"Oh gee, Mr. White, I'm not worthy"?

"I need a few more fights before I earn the public's acceptance to become the number one contender for Randy Couture's heavyweight title!"?

I took the opportunity that was presented to me, and I made the most of it. That's what a fighter does. That's what any businessman would do. Wouldn't YOU do that for YOUR family?

So many guys going into a big fight will screw themselves up in the head by listening to the critics and the so-called experts. Everyone was saying I didn't belong in that fight. That I didn't earn it. Randy has too much experience, I kept hearing. I, meanwhile, have no skills. But I never buy into the hype, the advertising, or the marketing. I ignore it all. When you step into the Octagon, hype means nothing. Reputations mean nothing. Nothing else matters but what happens when they lock that cage door.

It's just so pure. Two gladiators. One wins. One loses.

When the referee instructs the two warriors to "fight," the truth about a man is going to be revealed. Twenty thousand screaming fans. A worldwide pay-per-view audience. Everyone watching your every movement. Everyone wanting that spotlight to be on them at that moment.

If your instinct is to mind-fuck yourself, you're only setting yourself up for a loss. You either believe in yourself, and your camp, and your trainers, and who you are . . . and what you can do . . . or you don't.

By the time I was offered the title fight with Randy, I had moved up to Alexandria, Minnesota, which is about three hours northwest of Minneapolis. I set up my own training facility, the DeathClutch Gym.

I put my old wrestling coach, Marty Morgan, in charge of the camp. Greg Nelson and Erik Paulson came on board as my MMA trainers, and worked with me on my submission defense, striking, and general game plan. I was grappling with two-time NCAA Division I Champion Cole Konrad, and two-time NCAA Division II All-American Chris Tuchscherer. I brought in some other big, tough guys like Kirk Klosowsky and Jesse Wallace so I always had people who could push me harder and harder every day. When I needed work on specific skills, we would hire in the best people available, like seven-time Brazilian jiujitsu world champion Rodrigo "Comprido" Medeiros.

I actually like Randy Couture. Well, I like him now. I didn't let his status as a legend get into my head before we stepped into the Octagon with each other. Going into that fight, I kept reminding myself of the lesson I had learned against Wes Hand. I didn't want to have any respect for Randy at all. He was in my way, an obstacle to be overcome on my way to the UFC Heavyweight Championship. Randy Couture was preventing me from providing a better life for my family, and that's the only way I wanted to look at him.

When you step into the Octagon with Randy you are not just fighting him, you are fighting everything he's accomplished in the sport of mixed martial arts as well. It would be easy for anyone to be intimidated by his past, to be in awe of the fighter standing across the Octagon from you. But I knew that as soon as I thought to myself, "Oh wow, this is Randy Couture, he's this and he's that," I would be done. I would have already lost the fight, before it even started.

So I told myself, "I already know what Randy Couture is. Now I want to figure out what he isn't." That's the big difference between me and all of the guys that he beat. I didn't enter the Octagon holding Randy on some pedestal above me. I didn't even look at him as an equal. I looked at him as the guy I was going to beat. In my mind, I had no doubt that I was the better man, the more deserving champion.

As I stepped into the Octagon that night, the entire arena was booing me with a passion. It reminded me of my days as a heel in WWE. UFC fans did not want to see their hero crushed by a "fake" WWE professional wrestler. They wanted to see Randy show me that I didn't belong, beat my ass, and ship me back to Vince McMahon's doorstep in a box.

From the moment the crowd got their first glimpse of Couture, the chants of "Randy . . . Randy . . . Randy!" filled the arena. As much as the crowd was booing me, they were cheering for Randy Couture. I was loving every moment of it. I knew I was going to win. My training peaked just at the right time. My confidence was at an all-time high. I looked across the Octagon, and all I saw was the person I was going to smash and beat for the heavyweight title. I was minutes away from being able to afford the best life possible for my family.

During the first round, I listened to my trainers' advice, and just tried to feel Randy out. Could I get him up against the cage? Could I maneuver him? Was he leaving me any openings?

As I was feeling Randy out, he went to his old bread and butter, and tried to stand me up against the cage, where he could use his dirty boxing against me. But I saw it coming, shot on him, and took him to the ground, where I was able to control him. All three judges had me winning that round on their scorecards.

I came out for the second round, and caught Randy with a right hand, but he countered and caught me with a right of his own that opened up a cut above my eye. Randy saw the blood and thought he had me rocked, and he came in to finish the job. That's when I unloaded on him. I caught him behind the left ear with a solid shot, and he went down.

The moment Randy collapsed, I jumped right on him. I knew this was my chance to finish him off, and I wasn't going to let up until the referee, Mario Yamasaki, pulled me off and declared me the winner. I pummeled Couture unmercifully. It was just like going hunting. I was never going to give him a chance to escape. I just kept throwing my hands down on him as hard as I could. I could taste the victory, I could feel the victory was just moments away.

And that's when Yamasaki stopped the fight, and declared Couture unable to intelligently defend himself from my attack. The Legend had been defeated. I was the UFC Heavyweight Champion of the World!

Beating Randy Couture for the title was a great moment for me, but in the back of my head, all I could think of was getting my hands on Frank Mir again. As much as winning the title was the greatest professional moment I had experienced, losing that first UFC fight to Frank was still bothering me.

Meanwhile, the UFC was still going to crown an "Interim" Heavyweight Champion, and that guy was going to face me for the undisputed title. I have to hand it to Dana White and UFC match-maker Joe Silva, because they really knew what they were doing. The interim title fight was going to be between Antônio "Minotauro" Nogueira and . . . you guessed it . . . my old pal Frank Mir.

I really wanted to fight Big Nog, because he looked like the kind of fighter I would enjoy getting into the Octagon against. He's just an old-school fighter who enjoyed the battleground, the same type of warrior mind-set possessed by Randy Couture. But as much as I wanted to test my skills against Big Nog, I wanted to beat the shit out of Frank Mir even more. I needed to redeem myself against Frank. That loss to him was painful to me.

When Big Nog and Frank squared off, I was right in the front row, and I was cheering for Frank all the way.

From the first moment of the fight, I could tell Nogueira was sick. He should have been in bed, not in the Octagon. I'm not talk-ing about the guy having a cold or the sniffles or something, he was really ill.

What none of us knew at the time is that Nog had just battled a staph infection. When he got into the Octagon against Frank, he wasn't 100 percent. He wasn't even 50 percent. His reflexes weren't there, his reaction time was slowed, and he made Frank look like Muhammad Ali.

Frank Mir, the man who was born with a golden horseshoe up his ass, was once again handed a victory. He stood in the Octagon against someone who was much more of a man, much more of a fighter, than he could ever hope to be, and he got an easy knockout because his opponent had no business competing that night. Frankie Boy was crowned the UFC Interim Heavyweight Champion, and he should have retired on the spot, because his next step was to go up against me.

The UFC put the camera on me at ringside to get my reaction. I just smiled, and told the crowd that Frank had just given me an early Christmas present.

I don't know if Frank really, truly believed in his heart that he was going to be able to handle me the second time around, but I knew for an absolute certainty that I was going to beat him and get my redemption . . . and become the Undisputed Heavyweight Champion of the World.

My fight with Frank was scheduled for a few months down the road, but he had to postpone it due to a training injury. That turned out to be another lucky break for Frank, because he got to fight me for the undisputed title in the main event of the biggest mixed martial arts show of all time, *UFC 100*.

ROAD TO REDEMPTION

UFC 100 WAS scheduled for July 11, 2009, at the Mandalay Bay Events Center in Las Vegas, and my fight with Frank Mir for the undisputed title was the main event. I kept dreaming about what was going to happen in that fight, and I knew I was going to pull that golden horseshoe right out of Frank's ass and beat him over the head with it.

Frank went around bragging about how he had beaten me, which was one thing. But now he was walking around like it was a foregone conclusion that he was going to beat me again, and that he was already a champion. He's walking around with a fake title belt, and he thinks it carries the same meaning as the real title? Frank was lucky to get a fight with Big Nog for the fake title when Nog was sick as hell.

Frank was talking about how my punches felt like the ones his little sister would land after jumping on his back when they were kids.

Really? I had made hamburger meat out of his face during the eighty-five seconds I dominated our first fight, and now he's going to talk about me like I'm some bum? Frank was so arrogant, and it made me just want to punch him in the face so hard that I'd knock his head clean off his shoulders.

Even now, just thinking about him makes me want to hand a beating to Frank Mir again. And again. And again.

When I had to do the photo shoot with Frank for the very first *UFC Magazine*, I kept looking at him and asking myself, "How could I have given this guy a win? How could I let someone like THAT get their hand raised against ME?"

As soon as we started training camp, we put the pieces together on what it would take to beat Frank. It was easy to come up with a game plan because I knew in my mind that I had him beat the first time. I just had to control Frank, and it was obvious to me and my trainers that if I just got my hands on him, I could control him easily.

I wanted this fight bad, not just because I wanted to become the Undisputed Heavyweight Champion, but because I wanted the satisfaction of kicking Frank's ass. I wanted to beat him at his own game. I hated the fact that Frank was running his big fat mouth about how he was a great jujitsu expert, and about how he showed me the difference between jujitsu and wrestling, *blah blah blah*.

Frank claimed he was this great jujitsu black belt. What a crock of shit. Hey, let's face facts . . . when it comes to jujitsu, the truth is that a black belt doesn't mean a damn thing to me. Black-belt-fuckin'-schmack-belt. I'm a white belt, but I beat a black belt at his own game. Shouldn't that make me a black belt?

Frank submitted me because I made a stupid mistake, and all of a sudden he's the world's greatest submission artist. Sorry, everyone, but guys like Frank get awarded black belts based on how many hours they spend in the dojo. The belts come from the guys' own instructors. They don't have to beat anyone in a real fight in order to win them.

My coach didn't give me the NCAA Division I Heavyweight Title. I earned it. My training staff didn't award me the UFC Championship either. I earned both by kicking someone's ass for the honor of being champion. I deserved to be recognized as the best by beating someone man-to-man, in the spirit of competition. Frank got his black belt because he paid the instructor a lot of money over the years and put in his time. Big deal.

A lot of people talk about how I turned my back on Frank after the referee gave us our instructions in the middle of the Octagon. I guess we were supposed to touch gloves. I wasn't in the mood to touch gloves with Frank Mir. I had no desire to be respectful toward him. After all the shit he said about me, it was time for him to back it up. Hey, I said a lot of shit about him, too, and I was ready to back it up the moment the referee said it was legal for me to do so.

While we're on the subject of touching gloves and all that pageantry, let's get something straight. There are a lot of rules and regulations in the UFC, but touching gloves is not one of them. No state athletic commission mandates that fighters must touch gloves before they fight. So, in my mind, I'M NOT OBLIGATED TO TOUCH GLOVES OR HAVE A LICK OF RESPECT FOR MY OPPONENT, either before or after a fight. This is not a bunch of neighborhood kids all playing around on a bright sunny day in the backyard. This is a sport. At its very core, it's a fight.

I did exactly what I planned on doing in that fight. I took Frank down, controlled him, and hit him in the head repeatedly, and with violent intent. I scrambled his brains before the fight was stopped in the second round. I wish the referee would have let the fight go on a few seconds longer so I could have gotten the satisfaction of punching Frank in the face a few more times.

That win was very emotional for me. I had waited seventeen

long months to shut Frank's mouth, and it felt so good when I finally did it.

So there I am, in the Octagon, pumped full of adrenaline from the fight, crowd screaming, lights and cameras in my face, Frank in the corner with his face all messed up, and Joe Rogan sticks a microphone in front of me and asks, "Hey, Brock, how does it feel?"

How does it feel?

I've been waiting for seventeen months to punch this overhyped asshole Frank Mir in the face, use my wrestling skills to control his body, manhandle him like a bitch. I've been waiting seventeen months to prove to myself, the public, God, and everyone else who cares or doesn't care, that this guy doesn't measure up to Brock Lesnar. I've been waiting seventeen months to pull that golden horseshoe out of Frank's ass and beat him over the head with it.

That's when it all came out. All of the emotion. All of the pent-up anger.

First, I flipped off the audience with both hands, because they were still booing me. I didn't even think about it. I just did it. A little WWE left in me? A little bit of the heel wrestler? Maybe. Then Mir stumbled over to me. I was so amped up from the win, I failed to see that Frank was actually coming over to shake my hand. All I could think of was that I got the last punch in, and now I'm going to get in the last word. So I went nose-to-nose with him, got right back up in his busted face.

That's when I went on my tirade.

I don't know why, but I happened to look down and see the Bud Light logo on the Octagon floor, and it set me off. Bud Light was a UFC sponsor, and they had a lot of their people at the fight. But they weren't a Brock Lesnar sponsor, so I said I was going to celebrate by drinking "Coors Light, because Bud Light won't pay me anything." I also threw in "I might even get on top of my wife tonight."

Hey, Joe Rogan asked me how it feels.

Well, Joe, that's how it feels.

Dana wasn't happy. UFC owner Lorenzo Fertitta wasn't happy. My lawyers, who had been chased down the hall by Dana and Lorenzo and given a tongue-lashing, weren't happy. My own sponsors, sitting a few feet away, weren't happy. Hey, if it matters to you, I was pretty happy. Well, at least I was happy for a little while.

What was I supposed to say? "Congratulations to Frank Mir for a great fight"?

Are you kidding me? And besides, there is more to the story. I don't know how much trouble I'm going to cause by revealing any of this, but it's the truth, and that's why I'm telling this story in my book. If anyone has a different version, write your own damn book and tell the world how you see it!

About a month before *UFC 100*, Dana and Lorenzo flew to Minnesota to negotiate a new contract with me. My lawyers and I took them on a quick tour of the DeathClutch gym, then we went to a local resort to sit down and talk.

In addition to the contract, we discussed bigger sponsorship possibilities. I thought the UFC people were going to set something up for me before *UFC 100*, but we never heard anything about it again.

I don't know if I was supposed to be pissed about that, or if it's just one of those things. I'm not the easiest guy in the world to get along with. I'm also not someone who likes to be played, so the Bud Light thing was somewhere in the back of my mind during the fight with Frank Mir, and when I saw that logo on the Octagon floor, the trigger was tripped. Hey, I was on top of the world, looking down. And when I looked down, I saw that big Bud Light logo, and all that went through my mind was how much money UFC was making on that sponsorship, and how much I wasn't.

Everyone got a taste of Brock Lesnar that night. Unfiltered. I said what was on my mind. No script. No bullshit. Some liked what they heard, others didn't. I don't care.

Before the press conference that night, Dana took me into a bathroom and let me know what was on his mind. I said later that night that it was a "whip-the-dog session," and believe me, it was. Dana was trying to run a business where we could all make a lot of money together. He explained that pissing off major sponsors was not the way to do it. And just so I'm honest as hell here in my own book about it, let me say that he didn't phrase his explanation too nicely. He was upset with me, and the truth is, he had every right to be.

That was probably the quickest trip ever from top of the world to doghouse. By the time we worked our way from the basement of the arena up to the press conference, I had settled down, and the professional side of me took over (if there is one). I had found a Bud Light keg at one of the concession stands on the way up, and I picked it up and was going to carry it in on my shoulder, but Dana saw what I was doing and nixed that idea. I still think it would have been pretty funny. Just imagine the press we would have gotten if I had walked into the press conference with a Bud Light keg on my shoulder.

My lawyers put a Bud Light bottle in my hand before I walked into the press conference room, and I put it front and center by my microphone when I sat down to face the media. They all got a few good laughs out of that.

Because I'm a "real man of genius," I also apologized to Bud Light. I told them, "I'm not biased. I'll drink any beer."

I'LL BE THE first to admit, I was unprofessional that night. But despite all of the fallout from my outburst, I was as happy as I have ever been in my whole life. I had found a career that excited me, but that also allowed me to be with my family. I was married to the woman I loved and knew I'd happily spend the rest of my life with. Rena had just given birth to our son Turk, a healthy baby boy. I was making good money. I was supporting my family like I always wanted, and there wasn't anything we needed that we didn't have.

Life wasn't just good, it was great. This was the greatest time in my life.

And then I almost died.

WHAT IS WRONG WITH ME?

GOING INTO *UFC 100*, I was like a grumpy bear with a sore ass. Fight week is miserable, because I'm just sitting around, waiting to get into a fight with someone. The training is over. The work, for the most part, is done. I get phone calls from friends, asking "what's up?" Nothing's up. I'm just sitting around, waiting to step into a cage in front of millions of people, and either kick someone's ass or get embarrassed by my opponent. That's it.

The week of a fight is the longest week on the calendar for me. I spend my time trying to think about anything except what's on everyone's mind . . . THE FIGHT. There's nothing left to do, except drive yourself crazy waiting for that Saturday night, when you go to the arena and finally get to actually do what you've just spent months and months training for. The hay, as they say, is in the barn. But I have to go to press conferences and talk about the fight. I have to go to weigh-ins and talk about the fight. Reporters ask me the same questions over and over. My face is everywhere. I can't get away from it. Everywhere I look, everyone I talk to, it's always there.

I went to the movies eight times during the week of *UFC 100*. Matinees, nighttime movies, anything to escape the hype for a couple of hours. It's like the calm before the storm.

Marty Morgan is my head trainer because he's been around me for years. Marty understands me, which means he knows when to talk to me about the fight, and when to just leave me alone with my own thoughts. He knows when I need to be with my training partners, and he knows when I shouldn't have anyone around me. When another person knows you inside and out like that, he can't be replaced. He's the key, the glue that holds everything together.

Thank God my wife was mature enough to understand what I needed to do. She went through the last part of her pregnancy practically alone while I trained. But she understood, and she couldn't have been more supportive.

Coming out of *UFC 100* was a totally different deal. We were all on an emotional high. Even though I was the happiest I had ever been, I had to clear my head. I had to get out of fight mode, and back into the mind-set of just being a husband, and being "Daddy" to my kids.

That's the part people need to understand. Going into a fight, I'm Brock Lesnar, UFC champion, professional mixed martial artist. Pro fighter. But the minute the main event is over, I only want to spend time with my wife and kids and the rest of my family.

As soon as the post-fight press conference for *UFC 100* was over, we flew to Jackson Hole, Wyoming, and spent a week hiding out in the woods. We went to Yellowstone. I got to know my new son.

When we got back to civilization, I got word that Dana wanted me to defend the title against Shane Carwin.

I took the fight. Why? Because I've never turned down a fight with anyone the UFC has offered. You want me to fight Shane Carwin? Then I'll fight Shane Carwin. I'll fight Shane Carwin, and I'll defend my title against him the same way I plan on doing with every other top challenger you put against me.

But when I started training for the fight with Shane, I could feel that something was wrong. I was exhausted all the time. Tired. Worn out. No energy.

There were days when I would get home from training, and I literally could not get off the couch. I had been battling some stomach problems for a while, but I didn't think too much of them and just went on. That was a big mistake. I should have listened to my body.

Now I had a real problem. My health was getting worse by the day, and the fight was getting closer. I had to make a decision. I wanted to be fair to the UFC, because they were already promoting the fight. But I knew there was no way I could continue training camp and be in any kind of shape to fight. Something was wrong with me. Very wrong.

I'm not a quitter, so postponing the fight against Shane Carwin was one of the toughest decisions I've ever had to make. I talked it over with my wife, Marty, and my lawyers, and we all agreed I had no choice. I was sick, and I needed to take care of myself.

I went to the local doctor, and was diagnosed with mononucleosis. It made sense to me at the time. Training camp can wear you down. My immune system was fatigued. I was susceptible to something like mono; it happens to fighters all the time. This time, it was happening to me. Or so I thought.

I wasn't happy about letting so many people down, and I really wasn't happy about being sick, so I took my family on a trip to Canada. I figured we could spend some time in the wilderness, and I could rest and get healthy again.

Not long after we got to western Manitoba, I woke up in the middle of the night with the worst pain I have ever experienced. I never felt like that before. I was sweating buckets, just drenching the sheets, and I was delirious. I didn't even know where I was. I remember seeing Rena looking at me, and then I fell back asleep.

I woke up a short time after that, and told Rena I needed to get to a hospital.

Fast.

I couldn't stand up on my own. That says something right there, doesn't it? Brock Lesnar. The ultimate fighting champion. You know, Baddest Dude on the Planet. And I couldn't even stand up. Couldn't help myself. Couldn't get from the bed to the car to save my own life.

My brother Chad was with us, and he is big enough to carry me to the car. He loaded me in, and we took off like crazy men. But as fast as he was driving, I still felt like punching him in the face because it wasn't fast enough. Poor Chad. He could have put both feet on the gas pedal and redlined the tachometer all the way, and it still wasn't fast enough for me.

I was in so much pain, and I wanted help, but we were in the middle of nowhere. It may sound funny to you, but the Manitoba prairie is at least two hours from the nearest town of any size. The speedometer is only reading ninety-nine miles per hour, and I'm thinking of how I can fight through the pain and beat up my brother because he's driving at a snail's pace. At least that's how it felt to me.

We got to a hospital in a town called Brandon, and they put me on morphine right away. That took care of the immediate pain, but I still didn't know what was wrong with me.

After I stabilized a bit, the doctors took an X-ray of my stomach, but that doesn't show tissue, and doesn't give you a full view of what's going on. The doctors knew it, and wanted to do a CT scan, but they only had one machine at the hospital, and it was broken. They told me it would be fixed at 11 A.M. the following morning.

The morphine was giving me a terrible migraine. Eight hours come and go, and they still don't have the CT machine fixed. Talk about being in the wrong place at the wrong time. The worst part about it for me was the total lack of control.

You can call it ego, or cockiness, or arrogance, or anything else you want, but I'm used to being in control. Some people were meant to lead, others were meant to follow. I was born to take charge. It's not only what I do, it's who I am.

All morphined up in that hospital, I was helpless, and I was hating every second of it. Rena, who, unbeknownst to us, was pregnant with my third child, our second son, was sitting next to my hospital bed, watching the hours go by. She had never seen me like this. She was scared, but she was ready to spring into action the moment we made a game plan.

More time went by. Still no new part for the machine. My condition was getting worse. I didn't know if I was dying, but it sure felt like I was.

The hospital gave me more morphine, and started me on chicken broth. They wanted to get something inside me, some nourishment, but my body rejected the chicken broth and I started throwing up everywhere. I may have been all zoned out on morphine, but I could tell something was seriously wrong with me. When your body can't even handle chicken broth, you're in big trouble, but that was secondary to the fact that I had no clue what was wrong, since they couldn't get a picture of my stomach. The doctor didn't know either. He was waiting on the part for the machine. Time was slipping away, and I was wondering if I would ever make it out of that hospital alive.

I put my faith in the doctors at that hospital. I shouldn't have. It almost cost me my career. It almost cost me my life.

Another day goes by, and I'm still going downhill. I've been in the hospital all weekend, and they still don't have a CT scan. They keep telling me the part for the machine is coming, and that I just need to wait a little longer.

I'm more than a little concerned. How much longer is this going to take? Can you please be a little more precise than "We're waiting on the part" or "It'll be here very soon"? What's very soon? How much time do I have until you're going to need to cut me open just to keep me alive?

When I told Rena I was going to die waiting for them to fix the CT machine, we both knew what we had to do. I said, "Let's get the hell out of here." She was happy to hear me say this because she was thinking the same thing.

I called one of the nurses in and asked for more pain medication. What I didn't tell her is that I needed the pain medication because I was planning to bolt, and had a long drive ahead of me. Rena and I intended to get in the car and head for the U.S. border just as fast as we could go so I could get myself into a real hospital.

Before we left, however, we needed a plan. Bismarck, North Dakota, was the closest U.S. city, so I called Kim Sabot. His son Jesse had been my roommate in Bismarck State College. Kim had dealt with his own health issues over a long period of time, and he assured us that the hospital in Bismarck could take care of me.

Destination? Bismarck!

Rena wheeled me out of the Canadian hospital, got me into the passenger seat, and we were off. Like Chad, she was only driving ninety-nine miles an hour, which made me bat-shit crazy. The damn vehicle had a governor on it. It wouldn't go any faster.

It is a four-hour car ride to Bismarck from the Canadian hospital I was in, and the pain on that drive was unbearable. I have a high threshold for pain, higher than most guys, and I couldn't deal with it. It felt like I had taken a shotgun blast to the stomach, and then someone poured in some salt and Tabasco and stirred it all up with a nasty pitchfork.

Rena got me to Bismarck, and we could tell the people in the hospital were on point. Within twenty minutes, I was already getting a CT scan and antibodies. A few minutes later, the doctors diagnosed me with diverticulitis. I was told I had a hole in my stomach. I was being poisoned from the inside with my own body waste. No wonder I felt like death.

The Bismarck doctors knew who I was, and what I did for a living. That means they knew that cutting me open would end my career, and they did not want to do that if it could be avoided. The doctors made a decision.

They said I had eight hours. If the medication appeared to be working on the infection, they would give me some more time. If it wasn't working, they would be forced to recommend immediate surgery to remove a large chunk of my colon.

I spent the next seven hours in the hospital with a 104.3-degree fever. The doctors started discussing the surgery. It was becoming a life-or-death situation.

With fifteen minutes left to go, my fever finally broke. I didn't have to have the radical surgery. I got a reprieve.

If the doctor who made the decision to wait hadn't been on duty that day when I arrived, I would have been using a colostomy bag for several months, and would have had to undergo several surgeries. He made a brilliant decision. He and his twenty-eight years of GI experience saved my life . . . he gave me a chance to have a good life with my wife and children. I'll never forget that. Thank you, Dr. Bruderer. I will forever remember you for what you did for me and my family.

Although I had avoided immediate surgery, it didn't change the fact that I still had a hole in my stomach, and that it was slowly killing me. I was dying.

I spent the next eleven days in the hospital with no food or liquids. All I had was an IV solution and a ton of pain medication. I was living in a fog.

When I looked around, all I saw was my IV tubes and my wife sitting by my bedside. Rena tells me my lawyers were on the phone with her constantly, but I didn't know that. She tells me they had been in touch with Dana White, who offered to have a UFC helicopter take me to the Mayo Clinic. She tells me Marty was on his way. I didn't know that either. How could I know anything? I was so medicated I couldn't stay awake, and when I was awake, all I could think of was that I was dying.

One time when I woke up, I got ahold of my cell phone, and I started calling everyone . . . my managers, attorneys, trainers, you name it . . . and I fired all of them. If your number was on my cell phone, I either quit working with you or fired you.

Once I came to, I put those relationships back together. I was an ornery cuss when I was sick, and every now and then I have a good laugh about what I did from my hospital bed. It's funny, but not a lot of people on the other end of those phone calls have a sense of humor about it, even to this day. Oh well. I hope they get over it somehow. I'll admit, I was in a pretty bad mood, and had no idea what I was doing during most of those calls.

Rena just kept telling me to focus on positive thoughts, but while I was there in that hospital bed, I decided to retire. One of the people I called on the phone was Dana White. He's the one guy who laughs about the calls from me when I was in the hospital. That's just Dana's personality. I like that about him, because I'm sure he got an earful from me that week and a half I was laid up. I do remember telling Dana I was retiring. We both laugh about that conversation now. Not so much then. But certainly now.

I wanted to live. I wanted to get out of the hospital, and be with my family. Everything else was secondary to me. I was going to be a farmer. No kidding. Everyone still asks me if I was scared about losing my UFC career, never having a chance to see my title reign the whole way through. I wasn't that concerned about it, because when I was in that hospital bed, I had already resigned myself to the notion of being Farmer Brock.

At the end of my eleven-day hospital stay, I was wheeled out to my car because I was too weak to walk. And that's when it really hit me. Four months ago I was invincible, and now I'm in a wheelchair. I looked over at Rena and I said, "The world's baddest man, huh?," and I laughed.

Getting home that day was harder for me than being in the hospital. The pain meds were wearing off, and every time I moved, the pain got worse. I felt every bump in the road. But worse than any pain was thinking about the physical condition I was in. I didn't want to look in the mirror, because I was afraid I would not recognize the man looking back at me. I knew that I would have to face facts sooner or later. So, slowly, I made my way over to the full-length mirror in our bedroom. I stared at my reflection, not believing it was really me, and mumbled, "Oh yeah, I'm the world's baddest man. The ultimate fighting champion."

Rena was standing behind me, and I heard her whisper, "You are."

I was being sarcastic. She wasn't.

It was at that very minute when I turned the corner and decided that I was going to get back on the horse. No more feeling sorry for myself. It was time to take control of everything again. If I was going to retire, I was going to retire on my own terms, not because some stupid illness took me out.

A hole in my stomach. I still can't believe it.

A couple of weeks later, I went to the Mayo Clinic to get a complete evaluation. It usually takes a lot longer than that to get into the world-famous Mayo, but Dana called my lawyers with some contacts, and through those connections I was moved up on the list.

After what seemed like an endless series of tests, the Mayo doctors informed me that my best chance for a full recovery would be to have surgery. They wanted to remove about twelve inches of my colon. I wanted to know what my second-best chance was, because there is no way I was going to let them cut me up.

The doctors said I was out of immediate danger, so we could always do the surgery later. That was good enough for me.

I asked if I could exercise, and they told me it would be okay, as long as I didn't overexert myself. Of course, that meant I was in the gym the next day, but I was smart. All I did was walk on the treadmill a little bit. It beat the hell out of a wheelchair, and at least I was doing something.

You should have seen me. I looked like shit. I kept looking at an old picture of me when I wrestled in college at 260 pounds. I was lean and strong. Looking the way I looked in that picture again became my goal.

I had to get back into shape, and that meant a complete lifestyle change. It would defeat the purpose of my recovery to bulk back up, and end up with the same holes in my stomach that almost killed me the first time. I don't respect any of my opponents, but I have a lot of respect for diverticulitis. Me and diverticulitis went the distance, and I have no desire for a rematch.

I changed my diet completely. More vegetables. A whole lot more fiber. Nothing processed or preserved.

Then I started to do a little more in the gym each day. Cardio. A few light weights. A little more each day.

I approached my illness the same way that I approach a fight. I wanted to beat it. I wanted to take my illness down to the mat the same way I took down Frank Mir at *UFC 100*. I was in the fight of my life, and every day was another round.

When I returned to the Mayo Clinic for a checkup in January 2010, they gave me another CT scan. The doctors couldn't believe what they saw. They couldn't believe my stomach could heal without surgery the way that it did. They called it a remarkable recovery.

I wish I could express how that news made me feel. I didn't have to have my guts cut open. I didn't have to wear a colostomy bag. I could play with my kids, be the man that I was, only smarter, better, healthier. I had been given a new lease on life.

I was truly a man who had been blessed by God.

My wonderful wife showed me, once again, that she was going to stick by me no matter what. I had two healthy children, and had just learned that a third, my son Duke, was on the way. I was going to fight again. And now I had a newfound focus: I was determined to come back from my illness better and stronger than ever. Never again would I take the physical gifts God had given me for granted.

As much as I couldn't wait to get back into training and return to the Octagon, I want everyone to understand one thing. Yes, I wanted to be the greatest heavyweight the sport had ever seen. Yes, I was determined to come back stronger, healthier, more dominant than before. Yes, I wanted to prove to the world I was the greatest UFC champion of all time.

But what was most important to me was that I wanted to be a better husband to my wife and a better father for my children. It would be great to be the best UFC fighter ever, but none of that means anything without my family. They are everything to me, and they will always be my first priority. I hate what I went through, but it made me appreciate my family even more.

And so, with my family's support, I got ready for my comeback. If I could beat diverticulitis, there wasn't a man alive who was going to stand in my way.

THE LONG SHORT ROAD BACK

UFC WANTED ME to fight as soon as possible, but that meant waiting until the beginning of the summer. First, they had to crown another Interim Champion. That decision was made in December, when no one knew if I was ever going to be able to fight again. Dana, Lorenzo, and Joe Silva chose Shane Carwin and The Man With The Golden Horseshoe Up His Ass, Frank Mir, to fight in New Jersey at *UFC 111*. If the doctors had to perform the drastic surgery on me, that fight would have been to determine the new UFC Heavyweight Champion. If I could make it back, the Carwin vs. Mir fight would be for the Interim Championship, and the winner would face me for the real title mid-year.

I don't blame UFC for continuing to promote the Interim title fight even after I got clearance to return. You never know in the fight game. I could have gone back into training, and ended up right back in the hospital. That possibility was always looming. If they pulled the plug on the Interim title, and I got sick again, UFC would have to start all over, and that's a long time to go without a Heavyweight Champion.

I brought in Luke Richesson full-time as a strength and condition coach, and he turned out to be one of the most valuable members of my training staff, since his job was to rebuild me into a stronger but healthier athlete. Luke and I had been down this road before, when I was trying out for the NFL after messing up my body in that motorcycle crash. Here we were again, this time fighting back against my own body, which had attacked me from within.

Luke put me on a program and I started to gain lean muscle mass. I was feeling much healthier than before. I would joke around a lot about never eating my veggies before, but diverticulitis changed my outlook on a lot of things, and one of the important changes was that I was now watching everything that went past my lips. I worked hard for a lot of years to build up my body, and I ended up flat on my back, delirious, all drugged up on morphine because I got diverticulitis. When you quickly go from being a 280-pound warrior without a single doubt in your mind to being sick, helpless, and dependent, it better change your outlook or you haven't learned your lesson.

I learned mine. Period.

I didn't just want to rebound because of my fighting career. My son Turk was getting bigger and stronger every day, and I wanted him and my daughter, Mya, to grow up with a healthy father they could do things with. Rena was pregnant with our son Duke. I was motivated for a lot of reasons, but the most important reason I wanted to get back to being the "Brock Lesnar" that I knew was becuase my wife and children deserve the best.

UFC asked me to attend the Carwin vs. Mir fight so we could promote the Title Unification fight, which ended up being scheduled for July 3 in Las Vegas. I knew Dana and Lorenzo were happy, because either Carwin was going to knock Frank out and go to 12–0, so they could promote the Return of Brock Lesnar against this undefeated Knockout King, or Frank Mir would get lucky again, and we'd go for three, the big rubber match between me and Frankie.

Carwin knocked out Frank in the first round, and I can't say I'm surprised. Frank Mir was so obsessed with me, he was like a stalker. Everything in his life revolved around getting back into the Octagon with me, and he was looking right past his opponent. You can't do that, especially when you're fighting a guy with heavy hands like Shane Carwin.

Dana never told me he was going to call me into the Octagon when they were interviewing the winner of the fight, but I knew it was coming. The last time anyone had seen me in UFC was after I beat Frank, and I was giving the crowd the double bird and pissing off the sponsors. I wasn't looking for controversy with Shane Carwin, but I wasn't running from it either. When Carwin said winning the Interim Championship was this great big achievement, I just told it like it is. It's a fake title and that's a fake title belt. I actually felt bad for him if that was really the greatest moment in his life.

Training for Shane Carwin, we brought in Peter Welch, a famous boxing coach from Boston. Even though I broke Heath Herring's face with one punch and knocked out Randy Couture, I still hadn't learned the core basics in boxing. I wanted to find a grassroots boxing coach to help me learn how to get my feet underneath me. I had this great wrestling base, but how can I use that to my advantage, and combine my years of training as a wrestler with something as simple as a new stance so that when I punch, I'm punching from my feet to my hands. I wanted to learn the fundamentals, and Peter was the right guy to teach me these things.

Peter brings a lot of energy into everything he does, and that's infectious. He fit right in with my coaching staff. That's another key.

All of my trainers have to respect the fact that it's Marty Morgan who calls the shots. I've seen situations with other fighters where there are too many chiefs and not enough Indians. In my camp, Marty's the boss. We do things his way, because he knows what he's doing. He proved that to me at the University of Minnesota. J Robinson may have technically been the head coach, but Marty was the one who worked hard at developing that bond with me. Today it's no different. I trust Marty, because he's earned my trust. Peter Welch was used to running the show, but he adapted very quickly, and he became a huge asset.

With my wife pregnant, I knew I could ask for more time before I had to defend my title against Shane Carwin. Hell, I just came off my deathbed. UFC would have granted me any reasonable extension of time I requested, but I wanted to get back into the Octagon. It's the old expression about falling off a horse. You have to get right back on that pony and ride until you know you're the master again. I don't know how many more fights I will commit to in my fighting career, but I do know that when my career is over, it will be because I made the decision that my time was up. I'm not going to let fate make that decision for me. I want to see my career through to the end, on my own terms.

I felt the same way about Shane Carwin challenging me for my title. I just didn't see him as the guy to end my championship reign. I wasn't working this hard, sacrificing this quality time with my infant son, putting my wife through another pregnancy practically by herself, just to get knocked out by Shane Carwin.

We brought in a lot of wrestlers with heavy hands to mimic Carwin, because we knew that he not only had one-punch knock-out power but also was a Division II National Champion. I knew my wrestling was superior to his, but those hands were something to deal with. As long as I could avoid Carwin nailing me on the chin, there was nothing to worry about. I was determined not to get hit.

Right before the fight, referee Josh Rosenthal told us both, "This is for the UFC Heavyweight Championship, so I'm going to give both of you a fighter's chance. As long as you can answer my questions, and intelligently defend yourself, I'm letting the fight go on."

My biggest problem walking into the Octagon against Carwin was that I was so determined not to get hit, to avoid getting knocked out, that I stepped into the cage all tensed up. No matter who you are, or how tough you think you can be, that's a recipe for disaster. It actually almost cost me the fight.

That first round was a real test. Shane Carwin hit me hard, and he had me backpedaling. I had my bell rung, but I stayed calm. I don't know how to describe it, but all the time Carwin was pounding on me, it kind of woke me up, made me remember who I am. Was I nervous that Josh Rosenthal was going to stop the fight? Yes I was.

I was answering him, but I was also defending myself and watching for an opening to get out of the predicament. I couldn't hear my corner, and that's when a fighter finds out how much heart he has. All the training . . . all the trainers . . . all the sparring partners . . . all the sparring matches . . . none of it matters unless you have the heart of a champion. When you have a big strong athlete like Shane Carwin doing everything he can to knock you out, you can either fold under the pressure or weather the storm.

With every punch he threw, I could tell Carwin was shooting his wad. Each punch was a little lighter than the previous one. In many ways, that first round was exactly like my battle with diverticulitis. I just had to persevere. I was very fortunate that the fight wasn't stopped. I don't think it should have been, but there have been bad decisions made before.

When Carwin exhausted himself throwing punches one after another, I made my move. I got to my feet and muscled him up against the fence. I just wanted to survive that first round. It would sum up what I had been through the past eight months. I'd be able to get back to my corner and regroup, but it would also destroy Carwin's confidence. He hit me with everything he had and couldn't put me away. I could feel him breathing as I just pinned him up against the cage. He was done. No one had ever survived the first round with this guy, and I not only accomplished that, but I took everything he had and was still up on my feet controlling him as the round ended.

As soon as I got back to my corner, Marty asked how I was doing. I grinned at him, and said, "I'm doing great." Marty said, "Good, then put him away!" I had just taken a beating, but I felt fine, almost relieved. I was so concerned about getting knocked out after being out of the Octagon for a year, and now I knew there was no way my opponent was going to even luck into a knockout. There are two words that just don't go together in the English language . . . *TIRED* and *DANGEROUS*. Shane Carwin was tired.

Two minutes into the second round, it was all over. I got a take-down on Carwin, and forced him to tap to a choke. Just like *UFC 100* against Frank Mir, it was Comprido who came up with the strategy for how to finish off Carwin. We figured Carwin's camp was going to study whatever tapes they could of me, and there weren't many, because I only had four fights in UFC. Carwin was going to be careful about the half crucifix I used against Frank Mir. Comprido thought as soon as I took Carwin down and went for any kind of headlock choke, Carwin would get his arm in there, because that's the natural defense to the move. "He's going to want to get his body in toward yours," Comprido kept telling me as we worked on the variation of the choke over and over again in training camp, "but if you spread out, and use your wrestling base, you'll submit this guy."

When Joe Rogan interviewed me after the fight, I didn't say anything controversial. Like I always do, I spoke from the heart. "I am a man blessed by God," I told the world, and I truly felt that way. My wife was ready to give birth to my son Duke . . . I had come off my deathbed and defended my title . . . and I got through that first round beating to tap out Shane Carwin. I was in a great place. What more could I want out of life?

EPILOGUE

I T IS SUNDAY, March 20, 2011, and my deadline to finish this book is tomorrow morning. I was going to end it with a chapter about my fight with Cain Velazquez. But after all of these months, I've still never even watched the tape. I don't even want to think about it. I'm not ready yet.

I don't know how to approach it. A lot of things have crossed my mind. Part of me wants to move on and forget about it. But the athlete in me knows that I have to face my mistakes and learn from them if I want to get my title back.

I knew deep down inside that fighting Cain as soon as I did after the Carwin fight could have been a huge benefit to my career. But, with every benefit, there is a consequence. My consequence was a loss.

I'm human.

Yeah, I know. I'm not supposed to be, but I am.

I had been through a lot, some would even say "enough" in the year before the Cain fight. I got sick. Then worse. Then ended up in the hospital for eleven days with no food or water, being fed intravenously. Lost forty-two pounds. Had my whole life "on hold." Found out my wife was pregnant with another baby boy on the way. Got cleared. Did a minicamp. Tried to be there for my wife and Mya and Turk, but was all wrapped up in getting back into shape and getting ready for the Carwin fight. Did a full-fledged training camp, then fought Carwin.

After that, some downtime was overdue.

But I kept going.

Our son Duke is born. I have to tend to our farm, but something had to give. I am not a very good multitasker. I am a driven, focused individual. I had too much going on, and had been through too much for the entire year.

Why did I lose that night? Plain and simple. On that night, in that arena, Cain Velasquez was a better fighter than I was.

THERE'S AN OLD expression about falling off a horse. You get back on, and you ride that bad boy into town. I'm not saying I'm happy about losing the UFC Title, but I am saying it helped me focus again on how much I want to be champion.

In beating me for the title, Cain Velasquez tore his rotator cuff so badly he needed surgery and a year off to heal. Cain was scheduled to fight the number one contender, Junior Dos Santos, but that fight had to be postponed.

UFC knew both Dos Santos and I felt like the "Interim Title" was a fake championship, a placeholder until the real champ comes back. I made my feelings about that known when Shane Carwin was being called "The Interim Champion."

Dana and Lorenzo came up with a great idea, and made me an offer I couldn't refuse. If I agreed to coach on the *Ultimate Fighter* reality show, I would be set to fight the other coach in the end. I accepted, because the other coach was Dos Santos, and the winner of our fight gets Velasquez.

So I did what I had to do. I moved to Las Vegas for six weeks, brought my family with me, and coached a team of hungry young fighters. That put me on the fast track to get my title back.

I want to be the UFC Heavyweight Champion of the World again. There are also a few other things I'd like to take care of before I disappear and become Farmer Brock, but I like taking things one step at a time. The UFC title is in my sights. I need to pull that trigger first.

As for those other goals?

Well, we'll have to discuss those another time.

Maybe in *DeathClutch 2*!

ACKNOWLEDGMENTS

MY THANKS TO everyone who made this book worth reading, and my life what it is. My wife, Rena, and children, Mya, Turk and Duke; my mom and dad, for always being there; my brothers and sister; John, Jeff, Dick, and Alberta Schiley, for making me a part of their family; Bismarck State College and my coaches, Robert Finneseth and Ed Kringstad, my teacher Mary Ann Durrick, and my BSC teammates; Jesse Sabot, Mike Eckert, and their families; J. Robinson and Marty Morgan, for believing in me and pushing me to be my best; all of my UofM teammates, for going through it all with me; Brad Rheingans, my "brother"; Vince McMahon, for giving me my shot; Danny Davis, Gerry Brisco, Jack Lanza, and Jim "J.R." Ross; all of the boys I stiffed on the way in and out of WWE—keep your receipts and get in line; John Laurinaitis, for getting me the hell out of Louisville;

Dana White and Lorenzo Fertitta, for believing in me as an athlete; all of those who helped me along the way in my MMA career, Marty, Greg Nelson, Eric Paulson, Rodrigo "Comprido" Medieros, Luke Richesson, and all of the training partners who have pushed me and sacrificed for me; and my sponsors who have supported me.

I would also like to thank David Olsen, my longtime lawyer and manager, his colleague, Brian Stegeman, and their firm, Henson & Efron, P.A., for sticking with me in good times and in bad; Paul Heyman, for living some of the stories and writing this book with me; Scott Waxman, my literary agent; and Matt Harper, my editor, and the team at HarperCollins.

Special thanks to Medcenter One Hospital in Bismarck, North Dakota, the Mayo Clinic, and all of the extraordinary doctors and nurses who put up with me and made sure that I was alive to tell my story.

Thanks to you all, and to Webster, South Dakota, and all of the others who have played important parts in my life not mentioned here.